Chefs

Eat

Breakfast

Too.

DARREN
PURCHESE

Hardie Grant

BOOKS

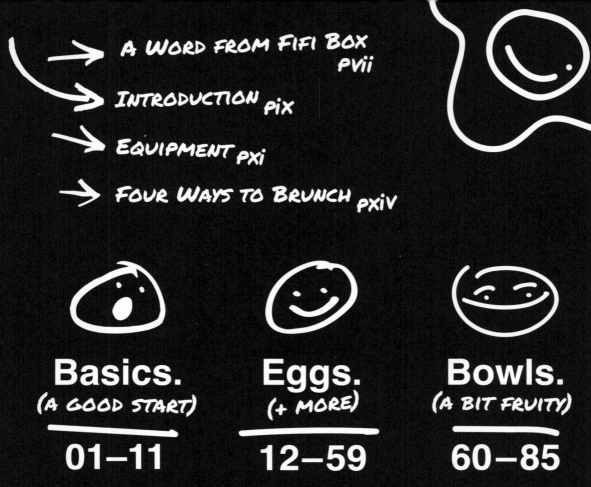

Basics.
(A GOOD START)

01–11

Eggs.
(+ MORE)

12–59

Bowls.
(A BIT FRUITY)

60–85

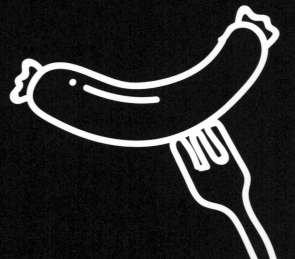

Sandwiches.
(+ OTHER WRAPPED THINGS)

86–109

Bressert.
(YOU SWEET LITTLE THING)

110–151

A word from Fifi Box.

From the moment I first met Darren on a cold winter's morning back in 2009 and he offered me one of his candied confections, making my nervous system tingle with excitement, I knew that I needed this man in my life. As a self-professed sweet tooth, I was aware that I had met the messiah of all things sugary and sweet.

When you taste Darren's cooking, you can taste his passion and love for the ingredients – his profound understanding of food and his respect for each element oozes from every mouthful. I have never witnessed a chef so committed to bringing joy to people through his food the way Darren does. For my daughter's first birthday party he created a chocolate fairy garden that blew the whole room away. Everyone was speechless. Each element was crafted so beautifully and curated with such love – it was so perfect I didn't want anyone to touch it. Every time my daughter went near it, I tried to distract her with a carrot stick!

Having worked in breakfast radio and television for many years, I am often reduced to eating my breakfast from a cardboard box, so when I heard Darren was writing a book of breakfast recipes I yelped with joy. Never again will I have to eat dry toast or lumpy porridge, because the master of all things yummy is sharing his wealth of delicious breakfast treats with everyone.

Thank you Darren for always putting one very special ingredient in all your recipes and everything you create: love.

Introduction.

Tired of dry toast? Bored with soggy cereal? Wanna make
breakfast like that 'so hot right now' cafe down the road? Well,
you've come to the right place. Going to one of those cafes on
a Sunday morning is like the new Saturday night; in fact, there
IS no going out on Saturday night anymore, 'cos if you sleep
in and arrive at the local brekkie hotspot after 8.30 am, you'll
probably end up queuing for lunch! Who needs the hassle?
Why not stay in those PJs and save that cash. Make your own
Insta-worthy breakfast at home and dazzle friends and family
with your new-found breakfast skills. How? This book has all
you need to start whipping up breakfasts to die for.

I have always loved breakfast; it's definitely one of my favourite
meals of the day to eat AND cook for. I have cooked many
breakfasts professionally in my time, from being brekkie chef at
some of the top hotels in London to making omelettes en masse
in France, to toasties here in Oz and lots more in between.
Although I have picked up tips, tricks and some exotic flavour
combinations on my travels, I still have a fondness for brekkie
classics, so here you'll find recipes such as the Perfect classic
omelette, Crumpets and Buttermilk pancakes, as well as dishes
such as Thai beef tartare w fried eggs and Chicken congee
w crispy doughnuts.

It really is worth going that extra mile for what's often referred to
as the most important meal of the day. And, these days, there
really are no rules about what you can eat: fish, meat, eggs, fruit,
veg – even bressert (breakfast and dessert) is now a thing…
You're welcome.

So get your day off to a great start and who knows what you can
achieve. Set that alarm and put the kettle on, get cracking (pun
intended) and open up a new world of brekkie possibilities. To
my mind, this is the ONLY cookbook worth getting out of bed for.

✳

This book uses 15 ml (½ fl oz) tablespoons; cooks with 20 ml (¾ fl oz) tablespoons should be scant with their tablespoon measurements.

It also uses metric cup measurements, i.e. 250 ml for 1 cup; in the US a cup is 8 fl oz, just smaller, and American cooks should be generous in their cup measurements; in the UK a cup is 10 fl oz and British cooks should be scant with their cup measurements.

Equipment.

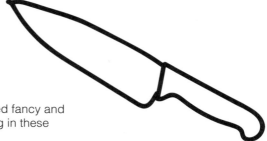

The best thing about breakfast is you don't really need fancy and expensive kitchen equipment. I recommend investing in these items but you won't need much more.

Digital thermometer
Take all the guesswork out of cooking times and cook with confidence. I use a digital thermometer for ease, and they are relatively inexpensive too. They are great for cooking caramels and syrups, for gauging oil temperatures when frying, and for savoury applications such as testing the 'doneness' of meat.

Microplane
I seriously could not live without one of these. I use them multiple times at work every day, and also when I'm cooking at home. They are great for zesting citrus rind and grating cheese (especially parmesan), and awesome for grating cloves of garlic instead of having to chop them.

Non-stick medium saucepans
These are perfect for scrambled eggs and poached eggs.

Digital scales
If there is a specific weight needed for a recipe, don't guess it, weigh it. You'll never look back once you start using these.

Mouli
This is a type of food mill with a handle that turns clockwise and coarsely blends soups, sauces and purées. I love using it for tomato sauces and ketchup because you don't have to peel the tomatoes, you can just push the mixture through it for a thick sauce.

Heat-resistant spatulas
These silicone spatulas are super handy for scraping mixtures out of bowls, leaving little to no waste. Or use them like wooden spoons for stirring when cooking. They are cheap and last virtually forever. To clean, just throw them in the dishwasher.

Omelette pan
I have a pan at home that I only use for omelettes, and I look after it by cleaning it by hand and not scratching the surface with anything abrasive. That way I know I will get perfect results every single time.

Piping (icing) bags
These are handy for all that cheffy stuff that goes on, such as filling doughnuts with cream, piping batter into muffin tins or for detailed work such as piping the crosses onto hot cross buns.

Smartphone
Use the timer on your phone when boiling eggs, or take a photo of all your hard work and upload that awesome breakfast pic to Instagram.

STRAWBERRY
CHEESECAKE
BRIOCHE P125

BREAKFAST QUICHE
P39

MEXICAN-STYLE
BAKED EGGS W
PICO DE GALLO
P52

CHOCOLATE,
YOGHURT
+ LEMON
CORNFLAKE
TARTS   P148

Four ways to brunch.

Go Thai

Thai beef tartare
<u>w</u> fried eggs **28**

Thai-style omelette
(khai jiao) **32**

Papaya smoothie
bowl <u>w</u> chia **67**

Honey nut
granola clusters **68**

Daz's Diner

Sausage <u>+</u>
egg muffin **101**

Anytime waffles
<u>w</u> bacon <u>+</u>
maple syrup **116**

Buttermilk pancakes
<u>w</u> lemon <u>+</u>
blueberries **120**

Red velvet
muffins <u>w</u> white
chocolate **151**

Basics.

(A GOOD START)

Basil pesto.

Makes 600 g (1 lb 5 oz)

2 large bunches fresh basil,
    leaves picked
275 ml (9½ fl oz) light olive oil
150 g (5½ oz) pine nuts, toasted
150 g (5½ oz) parmesan, finely
    grated with a microplane
1 garlic clove, finely grated with
    a microplane
finely grated zest and juice of
    ½ lemon
salt flakes
freshly ground black pepper

1/ Put the basil, 215 ml (7½ fl oz) of the olive oil, pine nuts, parmesan, garlic, lemon zest and lemon juice in a blender and blitz to a coarse paste. Season to taste with salt and pepper.

2/ Transfer the pesto to a container. Spoon the remaining oil on top of the pesto to prevent it from going brown. Cover and store in the fridge for up to 1 week, topping it up with a little more olive oil after each use.

Hummus.

Makes 400 g (14 oz)

180 g (6½ oz) dried chickpeas
pinch of bicarbonate of soda
    (baking soda)
2 garlic cloves, peeled
3 tablespoons tahini
3 tablespoons plain yoghurt
½ teaspoon cumin seeds,
    toasted and ground
juice of 2 lemons
salt flakes

1/ Put the chickpeas in a large bowl or saucepan and cover with at least three times the quantity of water. Stir in the bicarbonate of soda and leave to soak overnight. Drain off the water and rinse the chickpeas well.

2/ Put the chickpeas in a saucepan and cover with fresh water, then place the pan over medium heat and bring to the boil. Simmer for 1 hour, or until tender, skimming any impurities from the surface. Drain the chickpeas, reserving the cooking liquid.

3/ Put the chickpeas in a blender and blend for 5 minutes, or until you have a smooth paste. Use a little of the reserved cooking liquid to thin out the hummus to your desired consistency. Grate in the garlic using a microplane, then add the tahini and blend again for 30 seconds.

4/ Transfer the hummus to a bowl and stir in the yoghurt, cumin and lemon juice (don't add the lemon juice all at once, as you may not need it all). Season to taste with the salt. Adjust the flavour and consistency with more lemon juice, salt or tahini, to your taste.

Corn tortillas.

Makes 12

230 g (8 oz) masa harina flour
½ teaspoon salt
350 ml (12 fl oz) warm water

Chef's tip

Masa harina is a flour made from corn (maize) and used in Latin American cooking. Don't confuse it with cornflour (cornstarch) or cornmeal – you won't get the same results. It's available to buy online or in specialist ingredient and health food stores.

1/ Put the flour and salt in the bowl of a freestanding electric mixer and attach the dough hook. Turn the machine to low speed and add half of the water. Mix to form a thick paste, then add the remaining water in stages to form a smooth dough. Knead for a further 3–4 minutes and then remove the dough from the bowl.

2/ Divide the dough into 12 equal portions and roll each one into a small ball. Place a ball of dough on a plastic sheet (use freezer sheets or pieces of baking paper) and then place another plastic sheet on top. Sit a heavy-based saucepan on top of the dough and press the pan down to flatten the dough. The tortillas need to be 2–3 mm (⅛ in) thick. Use a small rolling pin to finish the job if necessary.

3/ Heat a skillet or heavy-based frying pan, without oil, over medium heat. Remove the plastic sheets from one of the tortillas. Place the tortilla in the pan and cook for 20 seconds, then flip it over and cook for a further 20 seconds. Continue to cook the tortilla for a total of 2 minutes, flipping it over every 20 seconds, until brown spots start to appear on each surface. Repeat the process to cook all of the tortillas.

4/ When cooked, stack the tortillas on top of each other and cover with a tea towel (dish towel) to stop them drying out. Use immediately or store in an airtight container in the fridge for up to 3 days or in the freezer for 2 months.

Tamari seeds.

Makes 250 g (9 oz)

100 g (3½ oz) pepitas
  (pumpkin seeds)
100 g (3½ oz) sunflower seeds
40 g (1½ oz/¼ cup) sesame
  seeds
80 ml (2½ fl oz/⅓ cup) tamari

1/ Combine the seeds in a dry non-stick saucepan. Place the pan over medium heat and toast the seeds, moving them back and forth in the pan until evenly toasted to golden brown.

2/ Remove the pan from the heat and add the tamari, stirring well to ensure the seeds are fully coated in the sauce. Leave in the pan to cool. Once cool, break the crunchy seeds into small pieces and store in a sealed container.

Dukkah.

Makes 250 g (9 oz)

100 g (3½ oz) hazelnuts
100 g (3½ oz) sesame seeds
25 g (1 oz) cumin seeds
25 g (1 oz) coriander seeds
salt flakes
freshly ground black pepper

1/ Preheat the oven to 180°C (350°F). Put the hazelnuts on a baking tray and toast in the oven for about 10 minutes, stirring them halfway through, until the skins start to split. Tip the nuts into a tea towel (dish towel) and rub off as many skins as you can. Chop or lightly crush the hazelnuts and transfer to a bowl.

2/ Place a small frying pan over low heat and lightly toast the sesame seeds, shaking the pan constantly to ensure they don't burn. Add to the bowl with the hazelnuts. Toast the cumin and coriander seeds, then tip into a mortar and pestle and lightly pound to break up the seeds a little. Add to the bowl.

3/ Season to taste with salt and pepper and stir to combine well. Store in an airtight container and keep in the freezer until needed.

Clarified butter.

Makes 200g (7 oz)

250 g (9 oz) unsalted butter

1/ Put the butter in a microwave-safe bowl. Cook in the microwave on High (100%) for 1 minute, then leave to cool in the microwave for 2 minutes. After this time the butter will have separated – use a spoon to skim off the foamy proteins from the surface and discard. Gently spoon the clarified butter into a clean container, leaving behind any water or milk solids in the bottom of the bowl.

2/ Alternatively, heat the butter in a saucepan over low heat until melted, then let it simmer until the foam rises. Skim off the foam with a spoon and drain off the clarified butter.

3/ Use clarified butter to make hollandaise or as a dipping sauce; it's also ideal for frying, as it can be heated to high temperatures without burning.

BASICS
4

Tomato ketchup.

<u>Makes</u> 1.3 kg (2 lb 14 oz)

1 kg (2 lb 3 oz) ripe tomatoes
60 ml (2 fl oz/¼ cup) olive oil
salt flakes
freshly ground black pepper
1 teaspoon fresh thyme leaves
½ teaspoon cloves
250 g (9 oz) brown onions,
    finely chopped
250 g (9 oz) peeled and diced
    apple
150 ml (5 fl oz) malt vinegar
125 g (4½ oz) jam setting sugar
pinch of cayenne pepper
1 fresh bay leaf

1/ Cut the tomatoes in half and put them in a microwave-safe dish (I like to use a glass Pyrex dish, which comes with a vented lid). Add half the olive oil, a good pinch of salt, some pepper and the thyme leaves. Place a lid on top and open the steamer hole. If your dish doesn't have a lid, use plastic wrap and poke a hole through the plastic to allow the steam to escape. Cook in the microwave on High (100%) for 15 minutes, then remove and set aside.

2/ Meanwhile, toast the cloves in a dry frying pan over low heat for 1–2 minutes until aromatic, shaking the pan constantly to ensure they don't burn. Cool, then tip into a spice grinder or mortar and pestle and grind or pound to a fine powder.

3/ Heat the remaining oil in a large cast-iron or heavy-based saucepan over medium heat. Add the onion and a pinch of salt and cook for 5 minutes to soften. Add the entire contents of the microwave dish to the pan, along with the ground cloves and all the remaining ingredients. Bring to the boil, then reduce the heat to low and cook for 1 hour, stirring occasionally.

4/ Blend the contents of the pan through a mouli (or use a blender) and transfer back to the saucepan. Cook over medium heat for 20 minutes, or until the sauce reduces to your desired thickness.

5/ Pour into hot sterilised jars and seal with the lids. Store in the pantry for up to 2 months. Refrigerate after opening and use within 2 weeks.

Guacamole.

<u>Makes</u> 450 g (1 lb)

2 ripe avocados
1 garlic clove, finely grated
    with a microplane
2 spring onions (scallions),
    trimmed and thinly sliced
finely grated zest and juice of
    2 limes
2 tablespoons chopped fresh
    coriander (cilantro) leaves
salt flakes, to taste
freshly ground black pepper,
    to taste

1/ Cut the avocados in half, discard the stones and scoop out the flesh with a spoon. Put the avocado flesh in a blender with the remaining ingredients and blend until smooth. Alternatively, use a fork to mash the ingredients together for a coarser consistency.

Darren's brown sauce.

<u>Makes</u> **1 kg (2 lb 3 oz)**

500 g (1 lb 2 oz) granny smith
    apples, peeled, cored and
    diced
250 g (9 oz) red onion, chopped
1 garlic clove, finely grated with
    a microplane
100 g (3½ oz) medjool dates,
    pitted and chopped
125 ml (4 fl oz/½ cup) water
250 ml (8½ fl oz/1 cup) apple
    juice
200 ml (7 fl oz) white-wine
    vinegar
50 ml (1¾ fl oz) malt vinegar
125 g (4½ oz/½ cup) tomato
    paste (concentrated purée)
125 g (4½ oz/½ cup) tamarind
    purée
50 g (1¾ oz) black treacle or
    molasses
½ teaspoon ground cloves
½ teaspoon ground anise
½ teaspoon freshly ground
    black pepper
½ teaspoon ground cinnamon
¼ teaspoon cayenne pepper
½ teaspoon allspice
50 ml (1¾ fl oz) apple-cider
    vinegar
salt flakes

1/ Put the apples in a large cast-iron pot or heavy-based saucepan. Add the onion, garlic, dates, water, apple juice, white-wine vinegar, malt vinegar, tomato paste, tamarind purée and treacle. Place over medium heat and bring to the boil. Reduce the heat to low and simmer the sauce for 45 minutes, stirring regularly. Remove from the heat and leave to cool for 30 minutes.

2/ Transfer to a blender and blitz until smooth. Tip the mixture back into the cleaned pot and add the ground spices and cider vinegar. Season to taste with salt. Return to medium heat and again bring to the boil, stirring regularly. Reduce the heat to low and cook, stirring, for a further 30 minutes.

3/ Ladle into hot sterilised bottles and seal with the lids. Store in the pantry for up to 6 months. Refrigerate after opening and use within 1 month.

Harissa.

2 red capsicums (bell peppers)
2 teaspoons cumin seeds
1 teaspoon coriander seeds
25 g (1 oz) red bird's eye
    chillies, chopped (with seeds)
2 garlic cloves, finely grated with
    a microplane
salt flakes, to taste

1/ Place the capsicums over the open flame of a gas stove burner (or use a kitchen blowtorch) and roast until the entire surface is charred and blistered. Transfer to a container, cover with a lid or plastic wrap and set aside for 10 minutes (the residual heat will steam the capsicums and loosen the skins). Use your fingers or a knife to rub or peel off the blackened skins. Roughly chop the smoky flesh and reserve.

2/ Put the cumin and coriander seeds in a dry frying pan and toast them over low heat, shaking the pan constantly to ensure the spices do not colour and burn. After 1–2 minutes, when their aroma has released, tip into a mortar and pestle and grind to a fine powder.

3/ Transfer the spice powder to a food processor. Add the capsicum pieces, chilli, garlic and salt and blend to a smooth paste. Store the harissa in the fridge for up to 1 week or freeze it in ice cube trays for up to 2 months.

Harissa vinaigrette.

Makes 180 ml (6 fl oz)

½ garlic clove, peeled
salt flakes
1 tablespoon Harissa (see
    recipe above)
35 ml (1¼ fl oz) white-wine
    vinegar
125 ml (4 fl oz/½ cup) light
    olive oil
freshly ground black pepper

1/ Crush the garlic with a pinch of the salt in a mortar and pestle until very smooth, then add the harissa. Use a fork or small whisk to mix in the vinegar and then the olive oil, and season to taste with salt and pepper.

Vinaigrette.

Makes 125 ml (4 fl oz/½ cup)

1 tablespoon sherry vinegar
2 teaspoons dijon mustard
salt flakes, to taste
freshly ground black pepper,
    to taste
finely grated zest of ½ lemon
100 ml (3½ fl oz) light olive oil

1/ Mix the vinegar with the mustard, salt, pepper and lemon zest. Slowly whisk in the olive oil to emulsify.

Soy dressing.

Makes 250 ml (8½ fl oz/1 cup)

100 ml (3½ fl oz) soy sauce
50 ml (1¾ fl oz) sesame oil
50 ml (1¾ fl oz) rice vinegar
50 ml (1¾ fl oz) water

1/ Put all of the ingredients in a small container with a lid. Seal and then shake the container for 1 minute to combine. Store in the fridge for up to 1 month. Shake before each use.

Thai dipping sauce.

Makes 140 ml (4½ fl oz)

2 tablespoons caster (superfine)
    sugar
3 tablespoons boiling water
2 tablespoons rice vinegar
2 tablespoons fish sauce
½ garlic clove, finely grated with
    a microplane
1 red bird's eye chilli, finely
    chopped (seeded if you
    prefer a milder sauce)
2 teaspoons lime juice
1 tablespoon finely chopped
    coriander (cilantro) leaves

1/ Put the sugar in a small heatproof bowl and pour over the boiling water. Stir until the sugar has dissolved. Add the remaining ingredients and stir to combine. Store in a jar in the fridge for up to 5 days.

Classic Seville orange marmalade.

<u>Makes</u> 4 x 450 g (1 lb) jars

2.25 litres (76 fl oz/9 cups)
   water
1 kg (2 lb 3 oz) Seville oranges
1 lemon
2 kg (4 lb 6 oz) sugar

1/ Pour the water into a large heavy-based saucepan. Cut the oranges and lemon in half. Squeeze the fruit halves and pour the juice into the saucepan. Reserve the juiced fruit halves.

2/ Set a 30 cm (12 in) square of muslin (cheesecloth) over a dish or bowl. Cut the squeezed fruit into quarters and then cut most of the pith and flesh away from the zest. Add the pith, flesh and any seeds to the muslin. Cut the zest into 5 mm (¼ in) strips and add to the pan, then scrape up any excess pith or flesh and place in the muslin. Use kitchen string to tie up the muslin into a loose bag and tie it to the handle of the saucepan so it hangs inside the pan, submerged in the liquid.

3/ Place the pan over medium heat and bring to the boil, then reduce the heat to low and simmer for 1 hour until the zest has softened. Turn off the heat. Lift out the muslin bag and carefully squeeze it to get all of the thick pectin syrup out and into the pan.

4/ Add the sugar to the pan and bring back to a rapid boil over high heat, stirring frequently. Cook the marmalade to 104°C (219°F); use a sugar or digital thermometer to accurately check the temperature. Be careful, as the marmalade tends to spit and splatter as the temperature increases.

5/ Remove the pan from the heat, ladle into hot sterilised jars and seal with the lids. Store in the pantry for up to 3 months. Refrigerate after opening and use within 1 month.

Strawberry jam.

Makes 3 x 280 g (10 oz) jars

500 g (1 lb 2 oz) strawberries,
*   fresh or frozen*
450 g (1 lb) jam setting sugar
½ lemon

1/ Put the strawberries and sugar in a heavy-based saucepan and mash the fruit with a fork. I prefer to use a cast-iron pan when cooking jam, as it retains the heat and doesn't stick as much.

2/ Place the pan over medium heat and bring to the boil, stirring the mixture frequently with a wooden spoon or heat-resistant spatula to ensure it does not catch on the base of the pan. Cook the jam to 104°C (219°F); use a sugar or digital thermometer to accurately check the temperature. Be careful, as the jam tends to spit and splatter as the temperature increases.

3/ Remove the pan from the heat and squeeze in the lemon juice through a sieve. Ladle into hot sterilised jars and seal with the lids. Store in the pantry for up to 3 months. Refrigerate after opening and use within 1 month.

White chocolate ± vanilla cream.

Makes 750 g (1 lb 11 oz)

500 ml (17 fl oz/2 cups)
*   thickened (whipping) cream*
1 vanilla bean, split lengthways
*   and seeds scraped*
250 g (9 oz) white chocolate
*   melts (buttons)*

1/ Put half the cream in a saucepan with the vanilla seeds and bring to the boil over medium heat. Remove from the heat.

2/ Put the white chocolate in a heatproof bowl. Pour the hot cream mixture onto the chocolate and leave to sit for 20 seconds before stirring to emulsify the chocolate. Add the remaining cream and mix well. Store the cream in the fridge for a minimum of 2 hours.

3/ Transfer the cream to the bowl of a freestanding electric mixer and attach the whisk. Whisk the cream on medium speed to firm peaks and use immediately.

Chocolate cream.

<u>Makes</u> 400 g (14 oz)

115 ml (4 fl oz) full-cream
   (whole) milk
115 ml (4 fl oz) thickened
   (whipping) cream
2 egg yolks
1 tablespoon caster (superfine)
   sugar
120 g (4½ oz) dark chocolate,
   roughly chopped

1/ Put the milk and cream in a saucepan over medium heat and bring to the boil. Remove from the heat.

2/ Combine the egg yolks and sugar in a heatproof bowl. Pour the hot milk mixture into the bowl and stir to combine well. Pour this back into the pan and return to a low heat. Stir the custard constantly with a heat-resistant spatula and cook to 82°C (180°F); use a digital thermometer to accurately check the temperature.

3/ Put the chopped chocolate in a heatproof bowl. When the custard has reached the correct temperature, remove the pan from the heat and strain the custard through a sieve onto the chocolate. Mix well with a whisk, then transfer to a container and refrigerate for a minimum of 2 hours before use.

Cream cheese frosting.

<u>Makes</u> 350 g (12½ oz)

225 g (8 oz) icing
   (confectioners') sugar
55 g (2 oz) cream cheese,
   at room temperature
55 g (2 oz) unsalted butter,
   at room temperature
1 tablespoon full-cream (whole)
   milk
¼ teaspoon salt
1 vanilla bean, split lengthways
   and seeds scraped

1/ Put all the ingredients in the bowl of a freestanding electric mixer and attach the paddle. Mix on low speed to combine, then gradually increase the speed to medium and mix for 1 minute. Stop the mixer and use a spatula to scrape down the side and bottom of the bowl. Mix again until the frosting is free of lumps.

2/ Transfer to a piping (icing) bag and use to pipe onto the Strawberry cheesecake brioche (page 125) or to top the awesome Red velvet muffins <u>w</u> white chocolate (page 151).

Eggs.

(+ MORE)

Filo-wrapped fried egg.

OMG, these are delicious! With the crunch from the filo, heat of the chilli, melted cheese and that runny egg, you'll be in breakfast heaven.

Chef's tips

Invest in a decent digital thermometer and you'll always have great results when frying (or baking). The oil temp is important: if it's too cold the filo parcels will be soggy and full of oil; if it's too hot they will burn and possibly split open.

There are many varieties of feta but I love Bulgarian feta. It has that great sharp tang typical of most fetas, but crumbles easily and melts away rather than keeping its shape.

Makes
4

Prep time
20 minutes

Cook time
12 minutes

4 large filo pastry sheets
160 g (5½ oz) unsalted butter, melted
80 g (2¾ oz) Bulgarian feta, crumbled
80 g (2¾ oz) gruyère, finely grated with a microplane
1½ tablespoons finely diced red onion
1½ tablespoons chopped fresh flat-leaf (Italian) parsley
1½ tablespoons chopped fresh coriander (cilantro) leaves
4 eggs, as fresh as possible
1 teaspoon Harissa (page 7)
4 teaspoons Dukkah (page 4), plus extra to serve
salt flakes
freshly ground black pepper
2 egg yolks, lightly beaten
1 litre (34 fl oz/4 cups) canola or sunflower oil, for frying

1/ Lay a sheet of filo on a work surface, with one of the longest sides closest to you. Lightly brush one half of the filo with melted butter and fold the other half over to create a double thickness rectangle. Brush the surface of the filo with more melted butter to prevent it drying out. Combine the feta and gruyère cheeses in a bowl. Take a quarter of the cheese mixture and arrange it in a circle, about 6 cm (2½ in) in diameter, in the centre of the filo – you are creating a well for the egg to sit in. Spoon a quarter of the onion around and on top of the cheese followed by a quarter of the parsley and coriander.

2/ Carefully crack an egg into the hole inside the cheese moat. Top the egg with ¼ teaspoon of the harissa, 1 teaspoon of the dukkah and season with salt and pepper.

3/ Lift up the bottom edge (closest to you) of the filo and bring it up and over the egg. Brush the left and then the right sides of the filo with the egg yolk and fold them into the middle, to stick to the bottom fold, then press down gently to stick the filo together. Brush the top of the filo, then lift it up and fold it towards the centre, covering the previous folds, to create a parcel. Brush the parcel with melted butter. Repeat with the remaining sheets of filo, the filling and eggs to make three more parcels.

4/ Heat the oil in a saucepan over medium heat to 180°C (350°F); use a digital thermometer to accurately check the temperature.

5/ Place one filo parcel into the hot oil and cook for 2–3 minutes, using a slotted spoon to gently flip it over in the oil to ensure even cooking. Remove and drain on paper towel. Repeat with the remaining parcels, cooking them one at a time. Sprinkle with extra dukkah and serve immediately.

Chilli scrambled eggs w̲ goat's cheese ± tomato.

There's nothing better than a hit of chilli to kickstart your day, and the addition of goat's cheese makes this breakfast dish one of my faves. Here the cheese helps to level the heat of the chilli and prevents the eggs from overcooking. I LOVE Meredith goat's cheese from Victoria; it's marinated in oil with herbs and a touch of garlic – I could put it on anything!

Chef's tip
Timing is everything when cooking eggs – start to cook them when the tomatoes are done and cooling. The toast needs to be coming out of the toaster at the same time as you're adding the goat's cheese to the scrambled egg. And put a couple of plates in the oven to warm up – there's nothing worse than breakfast on a cold plate.

Serves
2

Prep time
10 minutes

Cook time
15 minutes

10 or so tomatoes on the vine
80 ml (2½ fl oz/⅓ cup) olive oil (use the oil from the marinated goat's cheese if you like)
5 or 6 super fresh eggs
1 handful rocket (arugula)
2 tablespoons Vinaigrette (page 8)
2 slices bread (I used seeded sourdough), cut to 2 cm (¾ in) thickness
1 red bird's eye chilli, seeded and thinly sliced
80 g (2¾ oz) goat's cheese, marinated in oil
3 tablespoons finely snipped fresh chives
salt flakes
freshly ground black pepper
40 g (2½ oz) Tamari seeds (page 4)

1/ Preheat the oven to 180°C (350°F). Place the tomatoes on a baking tray, drizzle with a little of the olive oil and roast in the oven for 8–10 minutes until the tomatoes are cooked but not too soft. Turn the oven off and leave the tomatoes in there to stay warm while you prepare the rest of the dish.

2/ Crack the eggs into a bowl, ensuring there is no shell in the bowl, then set aside (don't whisk the eggs at this point). Put the rocket in a bowl, toss with the vinaigrette and refrigerate until needed. Place the bread into the toaster but don't drop the bread just yet.

3/ Okay, now the eggs. Heat a non-stick frying pan over medium heat. Add the remaining oil and then pour in the eggs. Instead of turning the heat up and down, you can control the cooking of the eggs by moving the pan back and forth from the stove top. Use a heat-resistant spatula to move the eggs back and forth gently; this is when you start to break down the eggs and mix the yolk into the white. You don't want the eggs to cook too fast; if they are, take the pan off the heat for a few seconds. Keep moving the eggs with the spatula until they start to thicken and look like scrambled eggs. Remove the pan from the heat and set aside.

4/ At this point, drop the toast and put the plates into the oven to warm through.

5/ Return the eggs to the heat and fold once more with the spatula. Add the chilli, goat's cheese and chives and remove from the heat. Fold again and then season to taste with salt and pepper.

6/ Place a piece of toast onto each plate. Spoon the scrambled eggs over the toast and then add the roasted tomatoes. Top with the dressed rocket and some tamari seeds. Serve immediately.

eggs 18

Soft-boiled eggs <u>w</u> anchovy toast.

One of my favourite foods as a child was a soft-boiled egg with toasted 'soldiers'. For me there is still something magical about pushing that first buttery, toasted soldier into the soft egg yolk and watching it burst up as you try to dip the toast into the yolk, without losing half of it down the side of the egg. Nowadays I love making this with anchovies, as I find their saltiness works so well with the eggs. I wonder if I would have eaten them this way when I was a kid?

Chef's tips
Get that egg right! For a perfect soft-boiled egg you need to gently drop medium, room-temperature eggs into a saucepan of simmering water and cook them for 5½ minutes. Use the digital timer on your phone for precision, and adjust future cooking times to the size of your eggs and past results. Serve immediately after cooking to ensure a runny centre.

I love anchovies and put them on just about everything, but there is a big difference between brands and quality. I prefer to pay a little extra and buy Ortiz anchovies, as the fish are superbly preserved, soft and free of small bones.

Serves
4

Prep time
5 minutes

Cook time
5½ minutes

100 g (3½ oz) unsalted butter, at room temperature
6 anchovy fillets, chopped
finely grated zest of ½ lemon
1 tablespoon finely snipped fresh chives
1 tablespoon finely chopped fresh flat-leaf (Italian) parsley
freshly ground black pepper
4 eggs, at room temperature
4 slices sourdough or white bread

1/ Put the butter, chopped anchovies, lemon zest and herbs in a bowl. Season with pepper and mix well with a spoon to combine.

2/ Bring a saucepan of water to the boil, then reduce the heat so the water is simmering. Gently drop the eggs into the water using a slotted spoon and cook for 5½ minutes.

3/ While the eggs are cooking, toast the bread and liberally spread the anchovy butter onto each slice. Cut the toast into 2 cm (¾ in) thick soldiers. Remove the eggs from the pan and cut open the tops using a knife. Serve in egg cups with the soldiers.

Perfect classic omelette.

The perfect omelette is a thing of beauty and is something that all good cooks should aspire to master. Omelettes can be cooked all the way through, but I prefer mine slightly runny in the middle with just a faint touch of colour on the outside. If you like, serve this with a simple herb or green salad tossed with my Vinaigrette (page 8).

Chef's tips

It shouldn't take long to cook an omelette – no longer than a minute to ensure the centre is still slightly runny. You don't want too much colour on the outside of your omelette either. Fillings are acceptable, but don't overdo it – keep it simple and ensure the ingredients are precooked if needed.

The art of the omelette flip onto the plate is worth practising for that restaurant-quality look.

Makes
1

Prep time
2 minutes

Cook time
1 minute

3 eggs, as fresh as possible, at room temperature
salt flakes
ground white pepper
Clarified butter (page 4), as needed
fresh chervil leaves, to garnish

1/ Crack the eggs into a bowl, season with salt and pepper, then lightly beat the eggs with a fork. Heat a non-stick frying pan over medium heat. When the pan is hot, use a pastry brush to brush clarified butter over the base of the pan.

2/ Pour the eggs into the centre of the pan in one go and leave them to set slightly for 10 seconds. Holding the pan with the handle, gently shake the pan while mixing the egg with a fork. Use the fork to pull the set egg from the side of the pan into the wet centre, and again leave to set for 10 seconds. Repeat the shaking of the pan and mixing of the egg with the fork. Cook for about 1 minute in total for a slightly runny omelette, then remove the pan from the heat.

3/ If you are right-handed, hold the pan in your left hand, with the handle away from your body, and tilt the handle up so the pan and omelette are angled downwards. Use the fork to roll the omelette over itself completely, from the handle side to the opposite side.

4/ Take a warm plate and bring the centre part of the plate to the edge of the pan, close to the omelette. Simultaneously flip the pan towards the plate and push the plate towards the pan, to flip the omelette onto the plate. This action will ensure the join of the omelette is underneath, leaving a perfectly rolled omelette. Brush some clarified butter over the top, garnish with a few chervil leaves and eat immediately.

Avocado ± Vegemite toast.

Vegemite, avo and coffee – what could be more Melbourne? My friend and awesome chef Kylie Millar caused an internet sensation last year when she pixelated avocado and posted it on her Instagram account @kyliemillar. She cut an avocado into tiny perfect dice with a super sharp knife and it was so awesome; it went nuts and now it's a thing. Search #pixelatedavocado. Awesome job Kylie; you are an inspiration to us all. x

Chef's tip
If you don't live in Oz then you're probably wondering, 'what the hell is Vegemite?' Well, it's a thick, spreadable yeast extract that has bags of umami flavour – people either love it or hate it. I LOVE it. Use Marmite if you're in the UK.

Serves
2

Prep time
15 minutes

Cook time
1 minute

2 slices sourdough or bread of choice
50 g (1¾ oz) unsalted butter, at room temperature
Vegemite, to taste
1 avocado, pixelated
½ lime
salt flakes
freshly ground black pepper

1/ Toast the bread under a hot grill (broiler) or in a toaster.

2/ Spread with butter followed by a thin layer of Vegemite – be careful, it's strong!

3/ Add the avocado, finely grate some lime zest over the avocado and then squeeze some lime juice on top.

4/ Season with salt and pepper.

5/ Take a picture.

6/ Post to Instagram. Watch as you get more likes than ever before.

Crumpets.

Being English I've always loved crumpets. They're sensational toasted and spread with lashings of cold butter, which then slowly melts and drips into the pillowy holes. Honey is my topping of choice but you can eat them with whatever you fancy.

Chef's tip
Get ahead of the crumpet game and make the batter the night before, then cover and pop it in the fridge overnight. In the morning, take the batter out of the fridge 20 minutes before cooking, and proceed from step 3.

Makes
8

Prep time
10 minutes (plus 1 hour resting)

Cook time
12 minutes

270 ml (9 fl oz) warm full-cream (whole) milk
2 tablespoons warm water
1 teaspoon caster (superfine) sugar
7 g (¼ oz/1 sachet) active dried yeast
230 g (8 oz) plain (all-purpose) flour
pinch of salt
canola oil spray
butter and honey, to serve

1/ Pour the warm milk and water into a jug and stir in the sugar and yeast. Leave in a warm place for 10–15 minutes, or until a thick frothy head has formed.

2/ Sieve the flour and salt into a bowl, make a well in the centre and pour in the yeast mixture. Mix the flour into the liquid and then whisk well to form a smooth batter. Cover with a tea towel (dish towel) or plastic wrap and leave to rise in a warm place for 45 minutes, or until light and frothy and doubled in size.

3/ Preheat a large non-stick griddle or heavy-based frying pan over medium heat. Lightly spray the griddle with oil, then place four 8 cm (3¼ in) crumpet rings or pastry cutters on the griddle. Spray the rings with oil spray, making sure they are well greased. Spoon some of the batter into the rings, filling each one about three-quarters full.

4/ Cook until bubbles appear on the surface and then burst, leaving holes, then turn the crumpets over with a palette knife and cook for a further 2–3 minutes. Transfer to a wire rack and remove the rings. Return the rings to the hot griddle, spray with oil again and cook the next batch.

5/ Serve the crumpets, lightly toasted if you prefer, with butter and honey.

Thai beef tartare w̲ fried eggs.

I've taken the classic beef tartare and upped it to 'next-level fabulous' by adding some awesome Thai flavours and a crunchy fried egg. Toasted and ground rice is added to the beef, which really adds an unexpected and delicious flavour.

Chef's tip
Use super fresh, great quality beef. Talk to your butcher and explain what you're making so they can give you the cut that's right for the dish.

Serves
2

Prep time
20 minutes (plus freezing)

Cook time
5 minutes

200 g (7 oz) fresh beef eye fillet or cut of your choosing
1 tablespoon raw jasmine rice
1 red bird's eye chilli, seeded and thinly sliced
2 spring onions (scallions), white part only, thinly sliced
1 handful fresh mint leaves, roughly chopped
1 handful fresh coriander (cilantro) leaves, roughly chopped
1 handful fresh Thai basil leaves, roughly chopped
½ Lebanese (short) cucumber, peeled, halved, seeded and cut into 5 mm (¼ in) dice
1 tablespoon sesame seeds, toasted
pinch of salt flakes
3 tablespoons Thai dipping sauce (page 8)
1 litre (34 fl oz/4 cups) canola or sunflower oil, for frying
2 eggs

1/ Put the beef fillet in the freezer for 30 minutes. Use a sharp knife to slice the beef to a 3 mm (⅛ in) thickness and then cut these slices into 3 mm (⅛ in) wide strips. Cut the strips into 3 mm (⅛ in) dice. Place in a bowl and refrigerate.

2/ Put the rice in a dry non-stick saucepan over medium heat and cook, shaking the pan, until the rice is evenly and lightly toasted. Tip the toasted rice into a small dish to cool down, then transfer to a mortar and pestle and grind into a powder.

3/ Transfer the diced beef to a large bowl, add the toasted rice powder and mix well. Add the chilli, spring onion, herbs, cucumber, sesame seeds, salt flakes and Thai dipping sauce. Gently toss all the ingredients together and then set aside.

4/ Heat the oil in a saucepan over medium heat to 180°C (350°F); use a digital thermometer to accurately check the temperature. When the oil reaches the correct temperature, reduce the heat to low.

5/ Crack the eggs into two separate small bowls. Pour one egg into the hot oil – it will sizzle and fry quickly – then use a slotted spoon to turn the egg over on itself, to keep it in a rounded shape. Cook for about 1 minute, then remove the egg with the slotted spoon and drain on paper towel. Cook the second egg in the same way.

6/ Divide the beef tartare between two serving bowls and top each one with a fried egg. Serve immediately.

PAPAYA SMOOTHIE BOWL W CHIA P67

HONEY NUT GRANOLA CLUSTERS P68

THAI-STYLE
OMELETTE
(KHAI JIAO) P32

THAI BEEF TARTARE
W FRIED EGGS
P28

Thai-style omelette (khai jiao).

This is such a cool technique for cooking an omelette and is super easy to whip up. I like to keep this simple and serve it with a few fresh herbs, some fragrant jasmine rice and Thai dipping sauce, which really makes this dish sing.

Chef's tip
Get the oil at the right temp and this is dead easy – and you certainly don't have to worry about the shape of this omelette either. Just take care when frying, as this can be a little unpredictable with spits and splatters of hot oil.

Serves
1

Prep time
10 minutes

Cook time
2 minutes

3 eggs
1 teaspoon lime juice
1 tablespoon rice flour
2 teaspoons fish sauce
1 tablespoon water
1 spring onion (scallion), trimmed and thinly sliced diagonally
400 ml (13½ fl oz) canola or sunflower oil, for frying
1 small handful baby coriander (cilantro) leaves
1 small bowl steamed jasmine rice
Thai dipping sauce (page 8), to serve

1/ Break the eggs into a bowl and lightly beat them using a fork. Add the lime juice, rice flour, fish sauce and water. Mix well again, ensuring all lumps have been removed. Add the spring onion and mix to combine.

2/ Heat the oil in a wok or large, wide saucepan over medium heat to 170°C (340°F); use a digital thermometer to accurately check the temperature. When the oil has reached the correct temperature, reduce the heat to low.

3/ Hold the egg mixture above the oil and pour it into the oil in one go. The egg will splatter slightly and puff up, but leave it to settle for 30 seconds, then flip the omelette using chopsticks or tongs and cook for a further 30–45 seconds. Remove the omelette from the pan and drain on paper towel for a few seconds before serving it immediately. Sprinkle with coriander and serve with a bowl of rice and the Thai dipping sauce.

Afghani eggs.

This is named after two Afghani kitchen hands who worked in my wife's Middle Eastern restaurant back in the early 2000s. This was their staple during Ramadan and they taught Cath how to make it, who in turn showed me. This is a favourite of ours when we get a day off together.

Chef's tip
Tabil is a spice blend originating from North Africa consisting of coriander and caraway seeds with chilli flakes or cayenne. It will lift the flavours in any dish, but works really well with tomatoes, eggs or as a dry rub for meats.

Serves
4

Prep time
20 minutes

Cook time
40 minutes

2 red capsicums (bell peppers)
4 tomatoes
2 tablespoons olive oil
1 red onion, cut into 1 cm
(½ in) dice
2 small garlic cloves, finely
grated with a microplane
2 red bird's eye chillies, thinly
sliced (remove the seeds if
you prefer mild)
Turkish bread or flatbread,
to serve
salt flakes
freshly ground black pepper
4 eggs, lightly beaten
3 tablespoons chopped fresh
coriander (cilantro) leaves

Tabil
1 tablespoon coriander seeds
1½ teaspoons caraway seeds
1 teaspoon cayenne pepper

1/ Place the capsicums over the open flame of a gas stove burner (or use a kitchen blowtorch) and roast until the entire surface is charred and blistered. Transfer to a container, cover with a lid or plastic wrap and set aside for 10 minutes (the residual heat will steam the capsicums and loosen the skins). Use your fingers or a knife to rub or peel off the blackened skins. Chop the smoky flesh into 2 cm (¾ in) dice and reserve.

2/ Score a cross in the base of each tomato with a paring knife. Plunge the tomatoes into boiling water and blanch for 20 seconds before removing with a slotted spoon and refreshing in iced water. Peel the tomatoes and discard the skins. Chop the tomatoes into 2 cm (¾ in) dice and reserve.

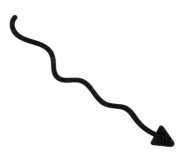

3/ Heat the olive oil in a large non-stick frying pan over medium heat. Add the onion and cook for about 10 minutes, or until completely translucent and soft. Add the garlic and cook for a further 2 minutes before adding the capsicum, tomato and chilli. Cook for 15–20 minutes, stirring occasionally, until the tomatoes have softened and you have a thick, rich sauce.

4/ Meanwhile, for the tabil, lightly toast the coriander and caraway seeds in a frying pan over low heat, shaking the pan constantly to ensure the spices don't burn. Transfer to a mortar and pestle and pound until finely ground. Add the cayenne pepper and mix well. Store any left-over tabil in a small plastic container for next time.

5/ Tear the Turkish bread into pieces and either char it on the stove top in a chargrill pan or cook it in the toaster.

6/ When the tomato sauce is ready, season it with salt, pepper and the tabil, to taste. Add the eggs to the pan and stir gently until the eggs are just cooked. Remove the pan from the heat and spoon the egg and tomato mixture onto plates. Sprinkle the coriander over the top and serve immediately with the charred bread.

Lightly fried egg <u>w</u> mushrooms, white anchovies ± crispy kale.

Cook your egg just like the fried egg emoji; that is, perfectly just set with no crispy bits or bubbles. I used nutty-flavoured pines and meaty brown mushrooms for this dish as they looked spectacular at the market that day, but use whatever you can find. The anchovies add luxury, the kale adds crunch and the pickled onion adds an acidic bite, all coming together for a real 'wow' dish.

Chef's tips

White anchovies (Spanish *boquerones*) are sensational and completely different to their tinned relatives. Unlike the tinned version, white anchovies are not cured in salt for a long time; instead, they are lightly brined and added to vinegar and oil (often flavoured with herbs or garlic) to produce a succulent flesh and a sweet taste. Buy them from good delicatessens or specialist food stores.

Pine mushrooms (saffron milk caps) are awesome in this dish. Buy younger ones if you can find them, as they have a delicate nutty flavour. Look for them when in season from late summer to early autumn.

Serves
2

Prep time
15 minutes

Cook time
15 minutes

½ red onion
1 teaspoon caster (superfine) sugar
salt flakes
2 tablespoons red-wine vinegar
400 ml (13½ fl oz) vegetable oil
10 small red and green kale leaves, washed and dried
100 ml (3½ fl oz) olive oil
2 pine mushrooms, stems removed, cleaned then halved or sliced
1 king brown mushroom, halved
50 g (1¾ oz) unsalted butter
freshly ground black pepper
2 eggs
8 white anchovy fillets

1/ Thinly slice the onion using a mandoline or sharp knife, then place in a bowl and add the sugar and ½ teaspoon salt. Mix well and leave for 10 minutes. Stir in the vinegar and set aside.

2/ Heat the vegetable oil in a saucepan over medium heat to 160°C (320°F); use a digital thermometer to accurately check the temperature. Add the kale leaves to the pan, one at a time, and fry for a few seconds until crispy. Remove the leaves with tongs and place on a tray lined with paper towel to soak up the excess oil.

3/ Heat half of the olive oil in a non-stick frying pan over medium heat. Add the mushrooms and a good pinch of salt and cook for 8 minutes, or until the sides start to caramelise, carefully lifting and turning over each slice with tongs. Add the butter and cook for a further 1 minute, then remove from the heat and season to taste with pepper. Pour the mushrooms into a dish.

4/ Use paper towel to wipe the frying pan clean and return to the stove top over low heat. Add the remaining oil and then crack the eggs into the pan (one on each side of the pan to keep them apart). Cook until the whites are almost opaque, then turn the heat off and allow the residual heat in the pan to cook the egg white to just set – the yolk should be bright and still runny.

5/ To serve, take two warm plates and use a spatula to place an egg in the centre of each plate. Arrange the crispy kale leaves, mushrooms, anchovy fillets and some pickled onion around the outside edge of the egg, leaving the yolk and most of the white fully exposed.

Breakfast quiche.

Okay, technically this isn't really a breakfast dish, as such. I often make a quiche for dinner, then refrigerate the leftovers and have it for breakfast the next day – I think quiche is sensational served cold. Of course you CAN make it on the day, but I'd suggest you make the pastry base the day before. This will give you a fighting chance of getting breakfast up before lunch!

Chef's tips

Getting that pastry base right is the key to a successful quiche: not too thin and not too thick, make sure it's cooked properly, and there are no holes for the custard to leak out.

You also want the eggs to be cooked perfectly. For best results, use a digital thermometer to ensure the filling is at the perfect setting point of 78°C (172°F).

Serves
8

Prep time
**20 minutes
(plus 30 minutes cooling)**

Cook time
1½ hours

1 x Shortcrust pastry base
(page 40)

Filling
50 g (1¾ oz) unsalted butter
50 ml (1¾ fl oz) light olive oil
4–5 leeks, white part only, sliced
(you will need 360 g/6½ oz
sliced leek)
180 g (6½ oz) Swiss brown
mushrooms, sliced
180 g (6½ oz) bacon, sliced into
thin strips
1 teaspoon chopped fresh
thyme
200 g (7 oz) gruyère, grated

Custard
350 ml (12 fl oz) full-cream
(whole) milk
10 eggs, lightly beaten
175 ml (6 fl oz) thickened
(whipping) cream
1 teaspoon salt
1 teaspoon freshly ground black
pepper
½ teaspoon freshly grated
nutmeg
½ teaspoon smoked paprika

1/ For the filling, heat the butter and olive oil in a large cast-iron pot or heavy-based saucepan over medium heat. Add the leek, mushrooms, bacon and thyme and cook, stirring regularly, for 15 minutes until the leeks and mushrooms are soft and most of the moisture has evaporated. Cook for a further 5 minutes if you think it needs it, then transfer to a dish and allow to cool for 10 minutes. Place the cooled filling into the prepared pastry base and spread it out evenly. Top with two-thirds of the grated cheese. Preheat the oven to 170°C (340°F).

2/ For the custard, heat the milk in a saucepan over medium heat. Meanwhile, combine the remaining ingredients in a large heatproof bowl or jug. When the milk starts to simmer, pour it over the ingredients in the bowl and blend with a hand-held blender. Pass the custard through a sieve into a jug.

3/ Place the quiche on the middle rack in the centre of the oven. Pull the rack out slightly and then pour the custard into the centre of the quiche, over the filling. Scatter the remaining cheese over the top, then gently push the rack and quiche back into the oven. Cook for 45–60 minutes, using a digital thermometer to check the internal temperature of the quiche. Once it has reached 78°C (172°F), the quiche will be cooked and set sufficiently.

4/ Leave the quiche to cool for a minimum of 30 minutes before cutting it. I like to leave mine overnight and have it for breakfast with a simple dressed salad.

SHORTCRUST PASTRY BASE

Makes
1 x 24 cm (9½ in) base

Prep time
20 minutes
(plus 1 hour chilling)

Cook time
35 minutes

*250 g (9 oz/1⅔ cups) plain
    (all-purpose) flour
125 g (4½ oz) unsalted butter,
    chilled and diced
1 teaspoon salt
1 egg
60 ml (2 fl oz/¼ cup) cold water
canola oil spray
2 egg yolks, beaten together*

1/ Put the flour, butter and salt in the bowl of a freestanding electric mixer and attach the paddle. Turn the machine onto low speed and mix until the texture becomes sandy and the butter is fully incorporated into the dough. Add the egg and water and continue to mix thoroughly to form a dough.

2/ Tip the dough out onto a lightly floured work surface and gently knead by hand to form a ball. Push the ball down to flatten slightly, wrap in plastic wrap and place in the fridge to rest for a minimum of 30 minutes.

3/ Lightly spray a 5 cm (2 in) deep, 24 cm (9½ in) springform cake tin with oil spray. Remove the dough from the fridge and leave it for 5 minutes to soften slightly before rolling it out with a rolling pin on a lightly floured work surface. Keep lifting the pastry to ensure it doesn't stick, using more flour as needed. Roll the dough out until about 3 mm (⅛ in) thick.

4/ Gently lift the pastry and place it into the centre of the tin, using your fingers to push the pastry into the base and around the side of the tin. Trim the excess pastry with a knife, but leave a little pastry overlapping the top of the tin (this will be trimmed off after cooking). Ensure the pastry is smooth, pushed into the side sufficiently and free of any holes or tears. If there are holes, use some of the excess pastry to plug them. Place the tin in the fridge for another 30 minutes to rest.

5/ Preheat the oven to 180°C (350°F). Line the pastry with a large piece of aluminium foil, pushing the foil into the side to fit the shape of the tin. Fill with baking beans, ceramic balls or uncooked rice to weight down the foil (use enough to fill to the top of the tin).

6/ Blind bake the pastry for 30 minutes. Remove from the oven and gently remove the foil and weights. Take a sharp paring knife or similar and gently trim the excess overhanging pastry from the tin. Return the pastry to the oven to dry out for a couple of minutes.

7/ Remove from the oven and brush with egg yolk. This will seal any tiny holes and help keep the pastry crisp. The heat of the cooked pastry will set the yolk immediately.

8/ You can now go ahead and make the filling, or leave the pastry base to cool, wrap in plastic wrap and use the next day (or freeze it for later).

Green eggs and ham w̲ tomato ± stracciatella.

The colours of Italy on a plate; this breakfast will have you thinking you've woken up in an Italian idyll.

Chef's tip

Stracciatella di bufala is a soft cheese made from Italian buffalo milk. When it's being made, the cheese is stretched to form long shreds, which is where the name originates. Ask your cheesemonger if it's available or see if you can order it in. It's well worth the trouble because it's rich, creamy, super spreadable and so yummy. If you can't find it, then a burrata or other soft cheese will do just fine, but you're guaranteed to experience major food FOMO.

Serves
2

Prep time
10 minutes
(plus 10 minutes resting)

Cook time
10 minutes

160 g (5½ oz) assorted tomatoes, cut into small chunks
1 tablespoon red-wine vinegar
salt flakes
freshly ground black pepper
4 eggs, at room temperature
2 tablespoons olive oil
2 slices olive bread, cut 2 cm (¾ in) thick
1 garlic clove, halved
100 g (3½ oz) stracciatella di bufala
4 wafer-thin slices prosciutto
4 tablespoons Basil pesto (page 2)

1/ Put the tomatoes in a bowl with the vinegar and season to taste with salt and pepper. Leave to sit for a minimum of 10 minutes at room temperature before using.

2/ Crack two of the eggs into two small saucers. Half-fill a saucepan with water, place over medium heat and bring to a simmer. Stir the water with a large spoon to create a whirlpool, then gently pour the eggs, one at a time, off the saucers into the centre of the whirlpool. Turn the heat off and leave the eggs to poach gently in the hot water. The eggs should be a perfect shape and set with a runny yolk after 4–6 minutes in the pan. Repeat the process to poach the remaining two eggs.

3/ While the eggs are poaching, brush the olive oil onto the slices of bread. Preheat a chargrill pan or barbecue grill to high. Char and toast the bread on both sides, then remove from the heat and rub the cut side of the garlic clove over one side of the bread. Put a slice of bread onto each warmed plate.

4/ Spoon or spread the stracciatella onto the toasted bread. Remove the poached eggs from the water with a slotted spoon and place on the plate. Add the tomatoes and prosciutto and spoon the pesto over the eggs. Serve immediately.

Mushroom, ham ± eggs benedict.

I've given the traditional eggs benedict a bit of a twist here with the addition of beautiful portobello mushrooms. Portobellos have a wonderful earthy and meaty texture, so you could easily leave out the ham if you wanted, but I have left it in. This is a breakfast classic for good reason: it's comforting and warming, and filling enough for you to probably skip lunch.

Chef's tip
It's a good idea to make the hollandaise sauce first before you start on the other components of the dish.

Serves
4

Prep time
10 minutes

Cook time
20 minutes

60 ml (2 fl oz/¼ cup) olive oil
4 portobello mushrooms, peeled
    and stalks removed
salt flakes
freshly ground black pepper
40 g (1½ oz) unsalted butter,
    plus extra for muffins
2 teaspoons fresh thyme leaves
4 very fresh eggs, at room
    temperature
2 English muffins (page 102),
    cut in half horizontally
4 slices shoulder ham
2 handfuls baby English spinach
Hollandaise sauce (see right),
    to serve

1/ Heat the olive oil in a saucepan over medium heat, add the mushrooms and season well with salt and pepper. Cook the mushrooms for 6–7 minutes on each side until caramelised, then add the butter and thyme to the pan. Cook for a further 1 minute, spooning the butter over the insides of the mushrooms. Remove the mushrooms from the pan and keep warm.

2/ Crack two of the eggs into two small saucers. Half-fill a saucepan with water, place over medium heat and bring to a simmer. Stir the water with a large spoon to create a whirlpool, then gently pour the eggs, one at a time, off the saucers into the centre of the whirlpool. Turn the heat off and leave the eggs to poach gently in the hot water. The eggs should be a perfect shape and set with a runny yolk after 4–6 minutes in the pan. Repeat the process to poach the remaining two eggs.

3/ Meanwhile, preheat the grill (broiler). Lightly toast both sides of the four muffin halves, butter them and place on four plates. Top each muffin with a slice of ham, some baby spinach and a mushroom. Use a slotted spoon to remove the poached eggs from the water and place them on the mushrooms. Spoon over the hollandaise sauce and serve.

HOLLANDAISE SAUCE

Makes
200 g (7 oz)

Prep time
10 minutes

Cook time
10 minutes

1 small French shallot, finely
  chopped
2 tablespoons white wine
1 tablespoon tarragon vinegar
2 tablespoons water
4 white peppercorns
1 small fresh bay leaf
2 egg yolks
150 g (5½ oz) Clarified butter
  (page 4)
1–2 teaspoons lemon juice
salt
freshly ground black pepper
1 teaspoon finely chopped
  fresh tarragon
1 teaspoon finely chopped
  fresh dill

1/ Put the shallot, wine, vinegar, water, peppercorns and bay
leaf in a saucepan over medium heat and cook until the volume
has reduced by two-thirds. Remove the pan from the heat and
allow to cool. Strain the mixture through a sieve into a heatproof
bowl. Add the egg yolks to the bowl and whisk by hand until the
mixture is foamy.

2/ Place a saucepan of water over low heat and bring to a
simmer. Set the heatproof bowl over the pan, ensuring the base
of the bowl isn't touching the water, and continue to whisk until
the mixture forms a thick ribbon when you lift the whisk from the
bowl. Keep an eye on the sauce at this stage; if it's getting too
hot the eggs will start to scramble.

3/ Very slowly at first, pour in the clarified butter in a thin, steady
stream while continuing to whisk vigorously and constantly.
Add in all of the butter and then remove the bowl from the heat.
Season to taste with the lemon juice, salt and pepper and then
stir in the herbs. Transfer the hollandaise to a serving dish. Use
immediately or cover and set aside somewhere warm.

Deep-fried eggs w̲ green sambal.

Dewi, our manager at B&P, is from Indonesia and she has very kindly shared her delish green sambal recipe with me, which she loves to eat for breakfast with deep-fried boiled eggs. This is great with rice for a bit more energy in the morning and to soak up every last bit of that amazing green chilli sambal. Thanks Dewi, you are awesome.

Chef's tips

You gotta cook that egg so the yolk is runny and that means about 5½ minutes. Refresh the eggs in cold water and then peel gently. Make sure each egg is completely dry before frying or the oil in the pan could splatter and burn you.

This makes more sambal than you need. Store any excess in a sealed container and refrigerate for up to 2 weeks. The sambal can also be frozen.

Serves
4

Prep time
10 minutes

Cook time
12 minutes

4 eggs, at room temperature
250 g (9 oz) long green chillies, halved and thinly sliced (with seeds)
4 French shallots, cut into 5 mm (¼ in) dice
2 green tomatoes, chopped
2 garlic cloves, finely grated with a microplane
1 teaspoon lime juice
2 kaffir lime leaves, thinly sliced
pinch of salt
2 tablespoons caster (superfine) sugar
60 ml (2 fl oz/¼ cup) olive oil
1 litre (34 fl oz/4 cups) canola or sunflower oil, for frying
steamed jasmine rice, to serve

1/ Bring a saucepan of water to the boil, reduce to a simmer and then gently drop the eggs into the water using a slotted spoon. Cook the eggs for 5½ minutes, then remove from the pan and refresh immediately under cold water for 5 minutes. Once the eggs have cooled, peel them and dry with paper towel. Set aside.

2/ Put the chilli, shallots, tomatoes, garlic, lime juice, lime leaves, salt and sugar in a large mortar and pestle and pound together to form a chunky sambal sauce.

3/ Heat the olive oil in a non-stick frying pan over medium heat. Add the sambal and cook for 5 minutes until fragrant and soft. Remove from the heat.

4/ Heat the canola or sunflower oil in a saucepan over medium heat to 170°C (340°F); use a digital thermometer to accurately check the temperature. Using a slotted spoon, drop the boiled eggs into the hot oil and cook for 45 seconds to 1 minute, using the spoon to gently move the eggs in the oil, until each egg has a crispy and light golden brown exterior.

5/ Divide the rice among four serving bowls, top with a deep-fried egg and some green chilli sambal.

Double eggy bread <u>w</u> shaved ham ± mustard.

Double egg! First the bread is soaked in a cheesy, eggy custard and then cooked with an egg in the middle. I'm a huge mustard fiend, so I love nothing more than slathering this with my fave dijon.

Chef's tip
Ask your favourite butcher (mine is Gary) to shave the ham as thinly as possible.

Serves
2

Prep time
15 minutes

Cook time
15 minutes

2 slices sourdough or bread of choice, cut 2 cm (¾ in) thick
4 eggs
125 ml (4 fl oz/½ cup) full-cream (whole) milk
75 g (2¾ oz) gruyère, finely grated with a microplane
2 tablespoons finely snipped fresh chives
salt flakes
freshly ground black pepper
75 g (2¾ oz) butter
120 g (4½ oz) ham, sliced wafer thin
mustard of your choice, to serve

1/ Preheat the oven to 180°C (350°F). Using a 5 cm (2 in) round pastry cutter, cut a hole from the centre of each slice of bread. Discard the small bread discs. Crack two of the eggs into two small saucers and set aside.

2/ Crack the remaining two eggs into a small bowl and add the milk, gruyère and chives. Season with salt and pepper, then mix with a fork to combine. Pour the custard into a shallow tray and add the bread slices. Leave the bread to soak for 3 minutes, then turn the slices over and soak for a further 3 minutes. Use a spatula to remove the bread from the tray and onto a wire rack. Place the rack over the tray and leave the bread to drain for 5 minutes.

3/ Place an ovenproof frying pan over medium heat, add the butter and cook until it just starts to froth. Cook the bread for 3–4 minutes, or until golden brown underneath, then flip the slices over and cook the other side for 3–4 minutes.

4/ Take one saucer of egg and gently pour the egg into the hole in the centre of the bread. Repeat with the second egg and remaining slice of bread. Cook for 1 minute, then transfer the pan to the oven and cook for 3–4 minutes to set the eggs. Transfer the eggy bread onto plates, top with ham and serve with some mustard.

Scuba's sweet potato hash browns.

'Scuba' Steve is my friend and fitness instructor and he's charged with keeping me fit and lean, especially after all of that doughnut testing (page 128)! We discuss breakfast ideas during workouts and he came up with this idea for the book, which I have to admit was pretty sensational – and they're delicious too. Each hash brown equals 50 burpees, so be warned.

Chef's tips

Start this recipe the night before and prepare the sweet potato up to the end of step 2. Cover the sweet potato in the tray and freeze for 4 hours or overnight, so it's ready to go first thing in the morning.

Make sure you use those biceps and squeeze all the water out of that grated sweet potato! No pain, no gain! You want the sweet potato to be as dry as possible, so the hash browns get nice and crispy when cooked.

Makes
20

Prep time
10 minutes
(plus 4 hours freezing)

Cook time
16 minutes

1 kg (2 lb 3 oz) orange sweet
   potato, peeled and coarsely
   grated
2 red onions, finely diced
2 tablespoons chopped fresh
   thyme
1 tablespoon finely chopped
   fresh flat-leaf (Italian) parsley
50 g (1¾ oz/⅓ cup) plain
   (all-purpose) flour
50 g (1¾ oz) butter, melted and
   cooled
2 eggs, lightly beaten
salt flakes
freshly ground black pepper
olive oil, for frying
poached eggs (see step 2, page
   43) and fried bacon, to serve

1/ Put the grated sweet potato in a large sieve and rinse well with cold water. Drain and then squeeze out the excess water (see Chef's tip). Transfer to a bowl and add the onion, herbs, flour, butter and eggs. Season with salt and pepper and mix well with a spoon.

2/ Lightly grease a 2 cm (¾ in) deep, 30 cm x 20 cm (12 in x 8 in) non-stick baking tray. Lay a piece of plastic wrap in the base of the tray and smooth it out with your hands to eliminate any wrinkles. Transfer the mixture to the tray and push down to spread and level it out. Cover with plastic wrap and place in the freezer for 4 hours.

3/ Lift the sweet potato slab out onto a chopping board. Remove the plastic wrap. Use a serrated knife to cut the slab into 20 rectangles, each 6 cm x 5 cm (2½ in x 2 in). Use as many hash browns as needed and store the remaining in the freezer for another time.

4/ Preheat the oven to 180°C (350°F). Line a baking tray with baking paper. Heat a little olive oil in a non-stick frying pan over medium heat and fry the hash browns for 5 minutes on each side until golden brown. Transfer to the tray and bake in the oven for 6 minutes, or until cooked through. Serve with poached eggs and bacon.

Mexican-style baked eggs w pico de gallo.

This is such a warm, nutritious and delicious start to the day. It's a take on the classic huevos rancheros but without the beans. It's perfect for any time of day but I love it for breakfast when I know I may not have time for lunch – it really keeps me going. Serve it in the pan for ease.

Chef's tips

Pico de gallo is a salsa-style dressing of zesty lime, crunchy onion pieces, beautiful tomatoes and herbaceous coriander (cilantro), and really gives this dish a lift. Use it on lots of other things too: to liven up a roast chicken or add a delicious oniony bite to tacos, or serve it as part of a dip selection with corn chips.

Use your knife skills to cut the ingredients into beautifully neat pieces, to add an Instagram-worthy fresh look to any dish.

Serves
4

Prep time
20 minutes

Cook time
40 minutes

6 tomatoes
1 fresh chorizo (about 180 g/ 6½ oz), casing removed and meat crumbled
1 tablespoon olive oil
1 red onion, halved and sliced
1 garlic clove, finely grated with a microplane
1 celery stalk, thinly sliced
1 yellow capsicum (bell pepper), seeded and thinly sliced
1 red capsicum (bell pepper), seeded and thinly sliced
1 teaspoon smoked paprika
1 long red chilli, sliced (with seeds)
4 Corn tortillas (page 3), cut into even-sized triangle pieces
4 eggs
2 spring onions (scallions), trimmed and thinly sliced
4 tablespoons chopped fresh coriander (cilantro) leaves
Guacamole (page 5) or avocado, to serve

Pico de gallo
6 ripe tomatoes, cut into 1 cm (½ in) dice
1 white onion, cut into 1 cm (½ in) dice
2 jalapeños, halved lengthways, seeded and cut into 1 cm (½ in) dice
1 handful fresh coriander (cilantro) leaves
2 limes
salt flakes

1/ Score a cross into the base of each tomato with a paring knife. Plunge the tomatoes into boiling water and blanch for 20 seconds before removing with a slotted spoon and refreshing in iced water. Peel the tomatoes and discard the skins. Chop the tomatoes into 2 cm (¾ in) dice.

2/ Place an ovenproof cast-iron skillet or frying pan over medium heat. Add the chorizo and cook gently, stirring regularly, for a couple of minutes to release some of the fat. Continue to cook until the edges of the chorizo start to caramelise.

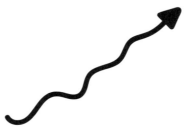

3/ Add the olive oil, onion, garlic, celery, capsicum and paprika. Cook for 10 minutes, stirring regularly, until the vegetables are soft and starting to caramelise on the edges. Add the chilli and diced tomato and reduce the heat to low. Stir and simmer for 20 minutes.

4/ Meanwhile, preheat the oven to 180°C (350°F). Lightly grease a baking tray and line with baking paper. Place the tortilla triangles on the tray and bake for 8 minutes, or until crisp. Remove from the oven and set aside. Leave the oven on.

5/ For the pico de gallo, combine the tomato, onion, jalapeño and coriander in a bowl. Use a microplane to grate in the lime zest, then cut the limes in half and squeeze in the juice. Season to taste with salt and transfer to a serving dish (serve at room temperature and make as close to serving as possible).

6/ When the tomato and chilli sauce is ready, remove from the heat and use a spoon to make four cavities in the sauce, evenly spaced apart. Crack an egg into each cavity and then transfer the pan to the hot oven. Cook for 5 minutes (or longer if you like your eggs firmer), then remove from the oven and sprinkle with the spring onion and coriander leaves. Serve with the crispy tortilla pieces, the pico de gallo and the guacamole.

Breakfast pizza.

I love pizza, but I especially love cold left-over pizza for breakfast when I am feeling a little seedy after a big night. I'm not talking about leftovers here, though. I am talking about a dedicated fresh pizza made especially for breakfast. Toppings are up to you but here's my ultimate breakfast suggestion. Now we're talking.

Chef's tips
Plan this well in advance, to give your pizza dough plenty of time to prove in the fridge. A slow and cold prove slows down fermentation, resulting in a better texture and flavour.

Get yourself an inexpensive pizza stone from a kitchenware store and pop it into your oven for an authentic 'cooked in a pizza restaurant' result.

Makes
1 pizza (serves 2), plus 1 extra base for freezing

Prep time
20 minutes (plus 2 days resting dough)

Cook time
7 minutes

Dough
250 g (8½ oz) strong (baker's) flour
140 ml (4½ fl oz) water
½ teaspoon active dried yeast
½ teaspoon salt
1 tablespoon olive oil
canola oil spray

2 pork sausages
2 eggs
150 g (5½ oz) pizza sauce
6 cherry tomatoes, halved
300 g (10½ oz) fresh buffalo mozzarella
4 thin slices prosciutto
small basil leaves, to serve
chilli oil or olive oil, to serve
freshly ground black pepper

1/ Make the dough 2 days in advance. Put the flour, water, yeast and salt in the bowl of a freestanding electric mixer and attach the dough hook. Mix on low speed for 1 minute, then increase the speed to medium and mix for a further 5 minutes. Turn the machine off and leave the dough to rest for 5 minutes. Turn the machine back on to medium and mix again. Add the olive oil and continue mixing for a further 5 minutes until the dough is smooth and elastic. Remove the dough from the mixing bowl and transfer it into a clean bowl. Lightly spray the surface of the dough with oil spray. Lay plastic wrap over the top of the dough and leave it to rest and prove in a warm place for 30 minutes.

2/ Line a tray with baking paper. Knock back the dough in the bowl by gently pushing it down with your knuckles. Transfer the dough to a very lightly floured work surface. Divide the dough into two equal pieces and roll each one into a ball. Place the dough balls on the prepared tray and lightly spray the surface of each ball with oil spray. Lay plastic wrap over the top of the dough to cover, then place the dough in the fridge for 2 nights.

3/ On the second morning, remove the dough from the fridge and leave in a warm place to prove and double in size. Preheat your oven (and pizza stone, if using) to 220°C (430°F), without the fan.

4/ Take a ball of dough, place it on a lightly floured work surface and gently knock it back again. Gently push and press the dough using the bottom of your palm to form a round shape, about 24 cm (9½ in) in diameter, lifting the dough every now and then to stop it sticking. Lift up the base again and flick some flour underneath before assembly.

5/ Use a knife to cut the casing from the sausages and crumble the meat into a bowl with your fingers. Crack the eggs into two small bowls.

6/ Top the pizza base with the pizza sauce, spreading it out evenly to cover. Add the crumbled sausage and tomato halves, then tear the mozzarella onto the pizza. Use a floured paddle to transfer the pizza to the pizza stone in the oven. Top the pizza with the two eggs and shut the door quickly. Cook for 6–7 minutes, then remove from the oven and transfer to a plate.

7/ Scatter some prosciutto and basil over the pizza and drizzle over some chilli oil or olive oil. Crack some black pepper over the top and serve immediately.

8/ Prepare and cook the remaining dough portion in the same way, but without the topping, then freeze it so you have a base ready for next time.

Spiced lamb pizza <u>w</u> fried egg, hummus ± lemon.

Picture this, if you will. Soft, pillowy home-made pita bread spread with delicious hummus, topped with fragrant spicy lamb, crunchy pine nuts and fresh mint, then all brought together with a runny egg and lifted with a touch of lemon and harissa-dressed coriander (cilantro) leaves. I would be happy with this every day.

Chef's tips

It's difficult to make pita in small quantities, so this recipe makes more than you need. This is all good; cook the remaining breads and then store them in the freezer for another time. To freeze the breads, stack them with baking paper in between each one, then cover and freeze for up to 1 month.

Shanklish is a hard cheese made from sheep's milk that is coated in a spice blend called za'atar. Look for it in specialist cheesemongers, food stores or Middle Eastern grocers. If you can't find it, then substitute with a hard feta cheese.

Serves
2

Prep time
10 minutes (plus 30 minutes resting)

Cook time
25 minutes

Pita breads
225 g (8 oz) plain (all-purpose) flour, unbleached
¼ teaspoon salt
¼ teaspoon caster (superfine) sugar
¼ teaspoon active dried yeast
2 teaspoons olive oil, plus extra for brushing
140 ml (4½ fl oz) warm water
extra flour, for dusting
canola oil spray

50 ml (1¾ fl oz) olive oil
125 g (4½ oz) minced (ground) lamb
1 long red chilli, sliced
1 garlic clove, finely grated with a microplane
1 teaspoon cumin seeds, toasted and ground
generous pinch of salt flakes
90 g (3 oz) shanklish, coarsely grated
60 g (2 oz) pine nuts, toasted
8 fresh mint leaves, thinly sliced
1 lemon, for zesting
2 eggs
4 tablespoons Hummus (page 2)
1 handful fresh coriander (cilantro) leaves
2 tablespoons Harissa vinaigrette (page 7)

1/ For the pita breads, combine the flour, salt, sugar, yeast, olive oil and warm water in the bowl of a freestanding electric mixer and attach the dough hook. Knead for 8 minutes on low speed, or until the dough is smooth and elastic.

2/ Line a tray with baking paper. Divide the dough into eight equal pieces and roll them into balls. Dust with flour and place on the tray. Lightly spray the dough balls with oil spray, then cover loosely with plastic wrap and leave to prove in a warm spot in the kitchen for 30 minutes, or until the dough doubles in size.

3/ Preheat a non-stick frying pan over medium heat. Roll out each ball on a lightly floured surface to an 8 cm (3¼ in) disc. Brush with olive oil and cook them, one at a time, in the pan for a minute or so. When the bread starts to fill with air and puff up, turn it over and cook the other side for the same time. Cook all of the breads, reserving two for breakfast. Freeze the remaining breads for quick meals another time.

4/ Heat half the olive oil in a non-stick frying pan over medium heat. Add the lamb, chilli, garlic, cumin and salt and cook for 6–7 minutes until the lamb is cooked through and has started to caramelise. Remove from the heat and add the cheese, toasted pine nuts and mint. Use a microplane to grate in the lemon zest, stir to combine and then transfer to a plate.

5/ Wipe the frying pan clean with paper towel and heat the remaining oil in the pan over low–medium heat. Crack the eggs into the pan and fry for a couple of minutes until cooked.

6/ Spread some hummus onto the pita breads and place on each plate. Spoon the lamb mixture onto the breads and top with a fried egg. Serve with the coriander dressed in the harissa vinaigrette.

Bowls.

(A BIT FRUITY)

Almond bircher muesli.

A great breakfast is always one that is easy to prepare – especially during the week, when you're trying to get out the door – and this gets no easier, because most of the hard work can be done the night before. I've made suggestions here so that this recipe can be adapted so it's suitable for vegans too.

Chef's tip
For best results use whatever fruit is in season. For example, switch the apples for peaches or apricots, or use cherries instead of raspberries. This combo works really well, but it's fun to experiment and come up with your own fave mixture.

Serves
4

Prep time
10 minutes (plus 20 minutes soaking and overnight refrigeration)

Cook time
Nil

- 225 g (8 oz/1¼ cups) rolled (porridge) oats
- 500 ml (17 fl oz/2 cups) full-cream (whole) milk (or almond milk)
- 1 apple, cheeks cut, coarsely grated with skin on
- 1 pear, cheeks cut, coarsely grated with skin on
- finely grated zest and juice of ½ lemon
- 2 tablespoons honey (or maple syrup)
- 30 g (1 oz) sultanas (golden raisins), chopped
- 30 g (1 oz) raisins, chopped
- 30 g (1 oz) almonds, roughly chopped
- 150 g (5½ oz) plain yoghurt (or coconut yoghurt)
- 1 orange, segmented
- 75 g (2¾ oz) strawberries, hulled and mashed with a fork
- 40 g (1½ oz) blueberries
- 80 g (2¾ oz) raspberries
- 50 g (1¾ oz) flaked almonds, toasted
- extra milk, to serve

1/ Combine the oats and milk in a bowl and leave to soak for 20 minutes. Mix the grated apple and pear in another bowl and stir in the lemon zest and juice.

2/ Now combine the soaked oats and grated fruit in a large bowl. Add all the remaining ingredients except a few blueberries, raspberries and the toasted flaked almonds, all of which will be used to garnish. Leave to soak and soften in the fridge overnight.

3/ Divide equally among four bowls and garnish with the reserved fruit and flaked almonds. Serve with a little extra milk to loosen the muesli to your desired consistency.

Coffee ± cacao maple granola clusters.

I love granola and make lots of versions depending on what I have to hand or how I feel. If I'm on the run and have to take breakfast with me, then granola is my go-to. To make it easy to transport, I put some yoghurt in a carry cup or container and add my favourite chopped fruit. I then cut a disc of baking paper, place it on top of the yoghurt and then put the granola on top of the paper; this ensures the granola doesn't go soggy. At my destination I remove the lid, discard the paper and am one spoon away from a delicious breakfast.

Chef's tip
This granola contains coffee beans, which will get you up and buzzing along. The coffee beans need to be blitzed in the blender until coarse but fairly small; don't leave them too big as they are very crunchy.

Makes
2.5 kg (5½ lb)

Prep time
20 minutes

Cook time
20 minutes

60 g (2 oz/¾ cup) roasted coffee beans
50 g (1¾ oz) puffed quinoa
80 g (2¾ oz) cacao nibs
600 g (1 lb 5 oz/6 cups) rolled (porridge) oats
400 g (14 oz) mixed seeds, such as sesame, sunflower and pepitas (pumpkin seeds)
100 g (3½ oz/⅔ cup) almonds, roughly chopped
100 g (3½ oz/⅔ cup) blanched hazelnuts, roughly chopped
100 g (3½ oz/1 cup) walnuts, roughly chopped
1 teaspoon ground cinnamon
1 teaspoon salt
150 g (5½ oz) unsalted butter
300 ml (10 fl oz) maple syrup
400 g (14 oz) mixed dried fruit, such as cranberries, apricots, sultanas (golden raisins) and currants, chopped
100 g (3½ oz/1¾ cups) flaked coconut
100 g (3½ oz) dark chocolate, chopped into small pieces

1/ Preheat the oven to 170°C (340°F). Line two 30 cm x 20 cm (12 in x 8 in) baking trays with baking paper.

2/ Coarsely blitz the coffee beans in a blender (see Chef's tip) and transfer to a large bowl. Add the quinoa, cacao nibs, oats, seeds, nuts, cinnamon and salt and stir to combine well.

3/ Melt the butter in a large saucepan over medium heat, then pour in the maple syrup. Bring to the boil and remove from the heat. Cool for 10 minutes before pouring onto the ingredients in the bowl. Mix well with a spoon or spatula (or use the paddle attachment from your electric mixer).

4/ Divide the mixture evenly between the two trays and spread it out to cover. Gently press down to compact (don't pack the granola too tightly or the clusters will be too thick and hard to break up). Bake both trays in the oven for 18 minutes, or until golden brown.

5/ Leave to cool in the trays and then break the granola into pieces into a large container. Add the mixed dried fruit, coconut and chocolate and mix well. Store in a sealed container in the pantry for up to 1 month.

Papaya smoothie bowl <u>w</u> chia.

Smoothie bowls are very on trend these days and their power-packed goodness will help put some pep in your step. The blended fruit is topped with soaked chia seeds – these tiny seeds are loaded with nutrients including protein, fibre and antioxidants. This is spot-on delicious and looks so professional, too. Hashtag smoothie bowl!

Chef's tips
Freshness is key here, so visit your local market and buy the best quality fruit you can afford.
   Prepare the strawberries, mango and banana the night before, then place into bags and freeze overnight so you're good to go in the morning.

Serves
4

Prep time
15 minutes (plus overnight freezing and 20 minutes soaking)

Cook time
Nil

200 g (7 oz) strawberries, hulled
150 g (5½ oz) mango flesh
1 banana, sliced
40 g (1½ oz) white and black chia seeds
350 ml (12 fl oz) almond milk
1 tablespoon maple syrup
2 large papayas, halved and seeds scooped out (reserve 1 tablespoon seeds)

Toppings
1 tablespoon toasted flaked coconut
4 strawberries, sliced
2 tablespoons pepitas (pumpkin seeds)

1/ Prepare the strawberries, mango and banana, place into containers or freezer bags and freeze overnight.

2/ The next morning, combine the chia seeds in a bowl with the almond milk and maple syrup and stir well. Leave the seeds to absorb the liquid and expand; this will take about 20 minutes.

3/ Meanwhile, take a small knife and a teaspoon and scoop out the papaya flesh from the four papaya halves to form a bowl shape. Put the scooped flesh and the reserved papaya seeds in a high-speed or bar blender. Add the frozen fruit and blend until you have a smooth and thick sorbet-style mix.

4/ Spoon the mixture into the papaya cavities and top with the soaked chia seeds. Top the bowls with the toasted coconut, strawberries and pepitas.

Honey nut granola clusters.

If you said to me: 'Darren, if you had to eat the same breakfast every day for the rest of your life, what would it be?' I would say: 'I'd eat this honey-baked granola with fresh fruit – preferably mangoes – and yoghurt.' That's more than enough introduction, I think.

Chef's tip
Freeze-dried fruit can be found online, from specialist ingredient stores and in some supermarkets. Once the packet is opened, seal it well to stop the product from attracting moisture in the air and going soggy, and store it in the fridge.

Makes
1.1 kg (2 lb 7 oz)

Prep time
15 minutes

Cook time
17 minutes

350 g (12½ oz/3½ cups) rolled (porridge) oats
50 g (1¾ oz) puffed quinoa
40 g (1½ oz) cacao nibs
100 g (3½ oz/⅔ cup) almonds, roughly chopped
50 g (1¾ oz/½ cup) walnuts, roughly chopped
100 g (3½ oz) sunflower seeds
100 g (3½ oz) pepitas (pumpkin seeds)
50 g (1¾ oz/⅓ cup) sesame seeds
pinch of salt
½ teaspoon ground cinnamon
½ teaspoon ground ginger
75 g (2¾ oz) unsalted butter
200 g (7 oz) honey
75 g (2¾ oz) dried cranberries
50 g (1¾ oz) sultanas (golden raisins), chopped
50 g (¾ oz/⅓ cup) currants
10 g (¼ oz) freeze-dried strawberry slices
50 g (1¾ oz/1 cup) flaked coconut

1/ Preheat the oven to 170°C (340°F). Line two 30 cm x 20 cm (12 in x 8 in) baking trays with baking paper.

2/ Put the oats, quinoa, cacao nibs, nuts, seeds, salt and spices in a large bowl and stir to combine well.

3/ Melt the butter in a large saucepan over medium heat, then add the honey. Bring to the boil and remove the pan from the heat. Cool for 5 minutes before pouring onto the ingredients in the bowl. Mix well with a spoon or spatula (or use the paddle attachment from your electric mixer).

4/ Divide the mixture evenly between the two trays and spread it out to cover. Gently press down to compact (don't pack the granola too tightly or the clusters will be too thick and hard to break up). Bake both trays in the oven for 12–15 minutes, or until golden brown.

5/ Leave to cool in the trays and then break the granola into pieces into a large container. Add the remaining ingredients and mix well. Store in a sealed container in the pantry for up to 1 month.

Berry smoothie bowl.

Are you serious? Anyone can make this super striking smoothie bowl. All you need is a decent blender to whizz everything together, then plate up like a pro with toppings such as fresh fruit, coconut, seeds or granola clusters.

Chef's tip
Peel and chop more fruit than you need for this recipe and store it in containers in the freezer. Then you can just blitz away whenever you want something quick for breakfast.

Serves
2–4

Prep time
10 minutes (plus overnight freezing)

Cook time
Nil

Smoothie
250 g (9 oz) blueberries
250 g (9 oz) pineapple flesh
2 bananas, sliced
1 orange, peeled and chopped
125 g (4½ oz) strawberries
125 g (4½ oz/1¼ cups) rolled
*   (porridge) oats*
125 g (4½ oz/½ cup) plain
*   yoghurt*

Toppings
fresh fruit such as raspberries,
*   strawberries or dragonfruit*
flaked coconut
pepitas (pumpkin seeds)
sunflower seeds
Granola clusters (page 64
*   or 68)*

1/ Put the blueberries, pineapple and bananas into containers or freezer bags and freeze overnight.

2/ The next morning, place the frozen fruit and all the remaining smoothie ingredients in a blender and blitz until smooth and thick. Transfer to a bowl and serve with toppings of your choice.

Coconut, turmeric ± ginger porridge w passionfruit ± banana.

Power up with this bowl of goodness – it will keep you happy until lunchtime. I prefer this served warm with fresh fruit, but it's just as good cold – make it the day before and loosen it in the morning with extra coconut milk.

Chef's tip
Fresh turmeric is readily available these days, as its nutritional benefits have been lauded in recent years. Find it in your local fruit and vegetable market or health food store – even some supermarkets now stock it.

Serves
4

Prep time
10 minutes (plus 15 minutes soaking)

Cook time
10 minutes

1 tablespoon grated fresh turmeric
1 tablespoon grated fresh ginger
500 ml (17 fl oz/2 cups) water
300 ml (10 fl oz) coconut milk
200 g (7 oz/2 cups) rolled (porridge) oats
2 tablespoons honey
1 vanilla bean, split lengthways and seeds scraped
pinch of salt
1 banana, sliced
2 passionfruit, halved and pulp scooped out
4 tablespoons shaved or grated fresh coconut
1 teaspoon ground cinnamon
1 teaspoon ground ginger

1/ Mix the fresh turmeric and ginger in a bowl, add the water and set aside for 15 minutes to infuse, or refrigerate overnight.

2/ Pour the turmeric and ginger infusion into a saucepan. Add the coconut milk, oats, honey and vanilla seeds. Place the pan over medium heat and bring to a simmer; cook for 8 minutes, or until the mixture thickens. Remove from the heat and stir in the salt.

3/ Divide the porridge among four bowls and top with the sliced banana, passionfruit, fresh coconut and a light dust of ground cinnamon and ginger.

FRUIT + NUT
BREAKFAST
BARS p142

COCONUT, TURMERIC
+ GINGER PORRIDGE
W PASSIONFRUIT +
BANANA p71

BERRY SMOOTHIE BOWL P70

TOASTED BREAKFAST BURRITO W SCRAMBLED EGG + AVOCADO P108

Quinoa porridge <u>w</u> peanut butter, banana ± coconut.

Healthy, delicious and easy to prepare, this is the perfect start to a chilly morning. I cook the quinoa in regular milk as I love the creaminess and flavour, but swap it for almond milk, soy or whatever you like if dairy is not your thing. A dollop of peanut butter is added to the porridge, and it's then served with sliced banana, honey and toasted coconut, though you can use whatever you fancy – try berries, toasted nuts or yoghurt. You could even stir in a spoonful of acai powder at the end of the cooking process for a superfood boost.

Chef's tips
Quinoa is gluten free, high in protein and contains all the essential amino acids. You can buy quinoa whole, puffed, precooked and in flakes, either from your local health food store or supermarket.

Toasting the quinoa flakes helps to remove some of the bitterness and adds a toasty flavour to the finished dish.

Serves
2

Prep time
5 minutes

Cook time
10 minutes

200 g (7 oz) quinoa flakes
25 g (1 oz) flaked coconut
500 ml (17 fl oz/2 cups) full-cream (whole) milk or milk of choice (almond, coconut, soy or oat)
2 tablespoons peanut butter, smooth or crunchy
1 banana, sliced
1 tablespoon honey

1/ Put the quinoa flakes in a dry frying pan over medium heat and cook for a few minutes, constantly moving the flakes in the pan until evenly toasted. Remove from the pan and allow to cool. Following the same method, lightly toast the flaked coconut.

2/ Put the milk and toasted quinoa flakes in a saucepan over low heat. Cook for 5–6 minutes, stirring regularly, until the mixture is thick and creamy.

3/ Remove from the heat and pour the porridge into bowls. Stir the peanut butter into each bowl and top with sliced banana. Drizzle with a little honey and sprinkle the toasted coconut over the top. Serve immediately.

QUINOA PORRIDGE

GREEN SMOOTHIE BOWL p76

Green smoothie bowl.

Anything green is generally very good for you, so why not combine all things green and good into a delicious and nutritious breakfast? This is especially great during the warmer months when you're looking for something light and rejuvenating to start the day.

Chef's tip
Follow my recipe or literally just go for it with your own favourite ingredients. Just remember to prepare your ingredients the night before and then freeze them overnight.

Serves
2

Prep time
10 minutes (plus overnight freezing)

Cook time
Nil

Smoothie
2 handfuls baby English spinach
2 kiwi fruit, peeled and sliced
2 green apples, unpeeled, core removed and chopped into chunks
1 avocado, halved, stone removed, flesh chopped into chunks
1 Lebanese (short) cucumber, peeled and sliced
2 bananas, sliced
1 handful ice cubes

Toppings
sliced carambola (star fruit)
sliced apple
pepitas (pumpkin seeds)
Honey nut granola clusters (page 68)

1/ Place all of the prepared smoothie ingredients (except the ice cubes) into containers or freezer bags and freeze overnight. Put two freezer-proof serving bowls into the freezer overnight.

2/ The next morning, put all of the frozen ingredients and the ice cubes in a high-speed or bar blender. Blend until the mixture is smooth, green and thick. Transfer to the chilled bowls and finish with the toppings from the list above, or toppings of your choice.

Chicken congee <u>w</u> crispy doughnuts.

You can eat congee any time of day but I love it for breakfast. It's warming, nourishing and packed full of flavour and is enough to keep you going until lunch. Congee is traditionally served with these yummy savoury fried doughnuts, *youtiao*. My mate and boss cook Poh Ling Yeow helped me with this recipe, and it's probably the most tested recipe in this entire book cos we just had to make sure. Thanks Poh!

Chef's tips

Cook the congee according to how you like the texture of your rice. If you like the rice grains intact, cook it for less time than specified, or cook it for a bit longer if you prefer the grains as they are starting to break down – or keep cooking to get a smoothish consistency with no notable grain (though you may need more stock or it could get too stodgy).

For the doughnuts, make the dough the night before and place it in the fridge for a slow prove, and to make life easier in the morning.

Serves
4–6

Prep time
15 minutes

Cook time
40 minutes

2 litres (68 fl oz/8 cups) chicken stock
10 g (¼ oz) fresh ginger, peeled and sliced
2 spring onions (scallions), trimmed and thinly sliced
200 g (7 oz) jasmine rice, washed and drained
2 boneless, skinless chicken breasts
2 chicken leg quarters (marylands)
1 teaspoon salt
Fried doughnuts (page 78), to serve

Garnishes
1 handful fresh coriander (cilantro) leaves
4 tablespoons fried shallots
light soy sauce
ground white pepper
sesame oil

1/ Pour the stock into a large saucepan and add the ginger, spring onion, rice, chicken and salt. Bring to the boil over medium heat, then reduce the heat to low and simmer for 30–40 minutes, stirring regularly, until the mixture has the consistency of a thick soup.

2/ Remove the chicken and use tongs or two forks to pull off and shred the meat, discarding the skin and bones. Return the shredded chicken to the pan and stir to combine.

3/ Spoon the congee into bowls and top with the garnishes. Serve with the crispy fried doughnuts.

FRIED DOUGHNUTS (YOUTIAO)

Makes
16

Prep time
20 minutes (plus resting and overnight chilling)

Cook time
16 minutes

185 g (6½ oz/1¼ cups) plain (all-purpose) flour
3 teaspoons baking powder
1 teaspoon caster (superfine) sugar
1 teaspoon salt
2 tablespoons vegetable oil
125 ml (4 fl oz/½ cup) cold tap water
canola oil spray
1 litre (34 fl oz/4 cups) canola or sunflower oil, for frying

1/ Sieve the flour and baking powder into the bowl of a freestanding electric mixer. Add the sugar and salt. Attach the dough hook and turn the machine onto low. Add the vegetable oil and then slowly trickle in the water. Increase the speed to medium and mix the dough for 5 minutes, or until smooth.

2/ Lightly spray the surface of the dough with oil spray. Lay a piece of plastic wrap on the surface of the dough and leave it at room temperature for 1 hour, then refrigerate overnight.

3/ Remove the dough and place on a lightly floured work surface. Push out with your fingers to form a 1 cm (½ in) thick rectangle measuring 20 cm x 10 cm (8 in x 4 in). Use a knife to cut the dough lengthways into two equal halves. Lay one half exactly on top of the other to form a 2 cm (¾ in) thick, 20 cm x 5 cm (8 in x 2 in) strip. Use the knife to cut this into sixteen 1–1.5 cm (½ in) thick strips.

4/ Place the doughnut strips on a tray lined with baking paper and use a floured chopstick to indent each strip lengthways. Leave them at room temperature for 30 minutes.

5/ Heat the canola or sunflower oil in a saucepan over medium heat to 175°C (345°F); use a digital thermometer to accurately check the temperature. Add four doughnuts to the oil (if the oil is at the correct temperature they will rise instantly) and cook for 3–4 minutes until golden brown and crispy. Use chopsticks or a slotted spoon to turn them over in the oil to ensure even cooking. Remove the doughnuts with tongs or a slotted spoon and drain on paper towel. Repeat with the remaining doughnuts.

Chicken ± egg rice bowl.

This is something you can easily knock up in the morning, as long as you have some dashi in the fridge. I like to make a decent-sized quantity of dashi so I can use it for other meals throughout the week. It's healthy and delicious and great on its own as a broth.

Chef's tips

The kombu, bonito, mirin, sake, soy, shiso and sansho pepper used in this dish can all be found at your local Japanese or Asian supermarket (there is usually one close by, especially in large cities). All of these will add authentic flavour to your Japanese cooking.

Mitsuba, which has a flavour similar to a mixture of flat-leaf (Italian) parsley and celery, may be harder to find because it's seasonal; if you're stuck, substitute with parsley.

Serves
2

Prep time
10 minutes (plus 1 hour soaking)

Cook time
15 minutes

Dashi
1.5 litres (51 fl oz/6 cups) water
10 g (¼ oz) kombu
40 g (1½ oz) dried bonito flakes

50 ml (1¾ fl oz) mirin
2 tablespoons sake
2 tablespoons light soy sauce
1 tablespoon caster (superfine) sugar
½ brown onion, sliced
1 tablespoon chopped mitsuba
2 spring onions (scallions), trimmed and thinly sliced diagonally
2 boneless, skinless chicken thighs, fat trimmed and sliced diagonally into 3 cm (1¼ in) pieces
4 eggs, lightly beaten
cooked short-grain rice, to serve
small red shiso leaves, to garnish
sansho pepper, to garnish

1/ For the dashi, put the water and kombu in a saucepan and set aside to soak for 45–60 minutes at room temperature. Place the pan on the stove top and bring to a gentle simmer over medium heat, then remove from the heat. Remove and discard the kombu. Leave the broth to cool for 5 minutes, then add the bonito flakes and leave to infuse. When the bonito flakes have sunk to the bottom of the pan, the dashi is ready.

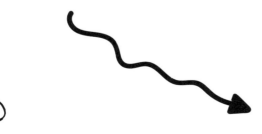

BOWLS
80

2/ Place a piece of muslin (cheesecloth) over a bowl and ladle and strain the dashi into the bowl. Discard the muslin and bonito and your dashi is ready to go. Dashi will last for up to 1 week in the fridge.

3/ Measure out 280 ml (9½ fl oz) of dashi and pour it into a bowl. Add the mirin, sake, soy sauce and sugar and stir to combine.

4/ Put the onion, mitsuba, half of the spring onion and the chicken in a saucepan and pour in the dashi mixture. Place the pan over medium heat and bring to a gentle simmer. Cover with a lid and cook for 4–5 minutes until the chicken is no longer pink. Remove the lid and pour in the egg, using chopsticks to gently move the egg around in the liquid. Keep the pan on the heat for a few minutes until the egg has just set.

5/ Divide the rice between two bowls and top with the chicken and egg mixture. Garnish with the remaining spring onion and the shiso leaves and sprinkle with sansho pepper. Serve immediately.

Quinoa, mushroom ± soy bowl <u>w</u> crispy fried egg.

Super healthy doesn't have to mean boring or bland; this breakfast bowl is delicious and will keep you going all morning. There are loads of great umami flavours happening here, and the seeds, veggies and crispy egg all combine to give a great crunch.

Chef's tip

Any mushrooms will do for this recipe, but I do love the look, flavour and textures of some of the Asian mushroom varieties. Look out for shimeji, shiitake, wood ear and enoki, but all mushrooms are fantastic.

Serves
4

Prep time
15 minutes

Cook time
25 minutes

90 ml (3 fl oz) light olive oil
4 spring onions (scallions), trimmed and thinly sliced
1 garlic clove, finely grated with a microplane
10 g (¼ oz) peeled ginger, finely grated with a microplane
180 g (6½ oz) quinoa, rinsed under cold water until the water runs clear
400 ml (13½ fl oz) hot chicken or vegetable stock (or hot water)
100 ml (3½ fl oz) Soy dressing (page 8)
2 sheets nori
300 g (10½ oz) mixed mushrooms
100 ml (3½ fl oz) soy sauce
80 ml (2½ fl oz/⅓ cup) rice vinegar
160 ml (5½ fl oz) sesame oil
4 eggs
100 g (3½ oz) Chinese cabbage (wombok), thinly sliced
1 carrot, peeled and julienned
2 tablespoons sesame seeds, toasted

1/ Heat 2 tablespoons of the olive oil in a cast-iron pot or heavy-based saucepan over medium heat. Add most of the spring onion (reserving some for garnish), the garlic and ginger and cook for a few minutes, stirring regularly, until softened. Stir in the rinsed quinoa, then add the hot stock and bring to the boil. Reduce the heat to low, cover with a lid and cook for 12 minutes, then turn off the heat. Leave to stand for 5 minutes before removing the lid. Season the cooked quinoa with the soy dressing and stir with a fork to combine. Set aside with the lid on.

2/ Using tongs, hold the nori over a low gas flame (or medium heat if your stove is electric) and toast it for a few seconds until dark green and crisp. Repeat with the second sheet. Tear the nori into pieces and reserve.

3/ Heat the remaining olive oil in a frying pan over high heat. Cook the mushrooms for 3–4 minutes until they soften and start to caramelise. Add the soy sauce and cook for 1–2 minutes until the soy has almost evaporated. Stir in the rice vinegar to deglaze the pan and then remove from the heat. Pour the mushrooms onto a warm plate.

4/ Wipe the frying pan clean with paper towel. Add the sesame oil and heat over medium–high heat. Crack the eggs into the pan and fry for a couple of minutes until the whites start to crisp up around the edges and the yolks are heated through but still runny. Remove from the heat.

5/ Divide the quinoa among four bowls and spoon the mushrooms and pan juices over the top. Add the sliced cabbage and carrot to the bowls, then top with a crispy fried egg. Sprinkle with the toasted sesame seeds, nori pieces and remaining spring onion. Serve immediately.

Sandwiches.

(+ OTHER WRAPPED THINGS)

Croque madame.

This sandwich – a favourite of mine – is definitely a knife and fork jobby! I make no apologies for being 'creative' with the traditional 'madame', adding in a tomato relish hit and LOTS of yummy herbs. Hot, crunchy, cheesy and oozy, this is the perfect start to the day.

Chef's tips

Get a head start by making the tomato relish the day before. If you like, you could prepare the recipe up to the end of step 4, then leave the sandwich to set in the fridge overnight.

I like to serve this with fresh herbs to really liven up the flavours. Look for chervil, chives, parsley, coriander (cilantro) or basil. Tarragon and dill can be great if used sparingly.

You won't need all of the relish and cheese sauce for this recipe, so store leftovers in the fridge (or freeze) for next time. Tomato relish is great to have on hand for many other things such as sandwiches, or use it instead of mustard with the Double eggy bread w shaved ham (page 48). Use the left-over cheese sauce in a lasagne or pasta bake.

Makes
2

Prep time
25 minutes (plus 50 minutes chilling)

Cook time
40 minutes

Tomato relish
250 g (9 oz) tomatoes, roughly chopped
2 long red chillies, roughly chopped (with seeds)
1 red onion, roughly chopped
1 garlic clove, finely grated with a microplane
150 g (5½ oz) soft brown sugar
2 tablespoons red-wine vinegar

Cheese sauce
500 ml (17 fl oz/2 cups) full-cream (whole) milk
50 g (1¾ oz) unsalted butter, softened
50 g (1¾ oz/⅓ cup) plain (all-purpose) flour
2 tablespoons dijon mustard
300 g (10½ oz) gruyère, grated
2 tablespoons chopped fresh tarragon
2 tablespoons finely snipped fresh chives
2 tablespoons finely chopped fresh coriander (cilantro) leaves
salt flakes
freshly ground black pepper

4 slices sourdough bread
4 slices smoked leg ham
1 tablespoon olive oil
2 eggs
assorted fresh herbs, leaves picked, to serve

1/ For the tomato relish, put all of the ingredients in a heavy-based saucepan over medium–high heat. Bring to the boil and cook for 10 minutes, stirring constantly with a heat-resistant spatula to ensure it does not stick to the pan. Remove the pan from the heat and leave the relish to cool.

2/ For the cheese sauce, heat the milk in a small saucepan and set aside. Melt the butter in a cast-iron or heavy-based saucepan over low–medium heat. Add the flour and cook, stirring with a heat-resistant spatula, for 1 minute. Slowly add the milk in a couple of stages, whisking the mixture to a smooth paste after each addition of milk. Reduce the heat to low and cook for 5–10 minutes, stirring constantly to stop the mixture sticking to the pan.

3/ Remove the pan from the heat and add the mustard and 100 g (3½ oz) of the cheese; stir well to incorporate. Mix in the chopped herbs and season to taste with salt and pepper. Transfer to a plastic container, lay plastic wrap on the surface of the sauce to stop a skin forming, and chill in the fridge for 30 minutes.

4/ Lay out the four slices of bread on a work surface and spread 2 tablespoons of the cheese sauce onto each slice. Top two slices of bread with half the remaining cheese and the ham. Spread some tomato relish over the ham and then close the sandwiches with the two remaining bread slices, placing them cheese-sauce side facing up. Scatter the remaining cheese on top of the sandwiches and refrigerate for 20 minutes to set (this could all be done the night before for a speedy breakfast).

5/ Preheat the oven to 180°C (350°F). Line a baking tray with baking paper. Place the two sandwiches on the tray and bake for 15 minutes until the bread is golden and the cheese has melted and is bubbling away.

6/ Meanwhile, heat the olive oil in a non-stick frying pan over medium heat. Crack the eggs into the pan and fry for a couple of minutes until the whites start to crisp up around the edges and the yolks are just set but still runny.

7/ Place the toasted sandwiches on two plates. Top with a fried egg and garnish with some fresh herbs.

Thick pork katsu sando.

You should know by now how much I love sandwiches, and when I hear of a new sandwich craze that's sweeping the world, I WANT IN! This sanga is Japanese in origin (and name), with *katsu* meaning cutlet and *sando* the Japanese abbreviation for sandwich. The crispy panko-crusted juicy pork is heaven and the fresh cabbage cuts through the fat; then, in a nod to a western bacon sandwich, it has my brown sauce blended with Japanese Kewpie mayo. But the real star is possibly that pillowy, thick crustless white bread. You seriously could eat this any time of day, but it certainly covers all bases for breakfast.

Chef's tip
Three things on your shopping list will make this dish soar:

1. You need fluffy, spongy sliced white bread – something that has been enriched with butter and milk is perfect. Try a Japanese-style bakery.

2. Kewpie mayonnaise: there is no substitute for this.

3. Panko breadcrumbs: one of Japan's greatest culinary gifts to the world.

Makes
1

Prep time
10 minutes

Cook time
12 minutes (plus 10 minutes resting)

50 g (1¾ oz/⅓ cup) plain (all-purpose) flour
salt flakes
freshly ground black pepper
60 ml (2 fl oz/¼ cup) full-cream (whole) milk
1 egg
50 g (1¾ oz) panko breadcrumbs
200 g (7 oz) pork loin, thick piece
2 tablespoons olive oil
25 g (1 oz) unsalted butter
100 g (3½ oz) Chinese cabbage (wombok)
50 g (1¾ oz) Kewpie mayonnaise
30 g (1 oz) Darren's brown sauce (page 6)
2 slices white sandwich bread, crusts removed

1/ Put the flour on a flat tray or plate and season it with salt and pepper. Combine the milk and egg in a small bowl and use a fork to mix them together. Put the breadcrumbs on a separate tray.

2/ Coat the pork loin in the seasoned flour and shake away any excess. Dip the pork into the milk and egg mixture, letting the excess drip back into the bowl, then dip it into the breadcrumbs, ensuring it is evenly coated. Shake off any excess breadcrumbs.

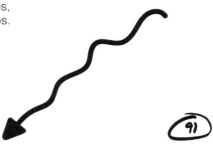

3/ Preheat the oven to 180°C (350°F). Heat the oil and butter in an ovenproof frying pan over medium heat. When the butter starts to foam, add the pork loin to the pan and cook for about 3 minutes until the breadcrumbs are golden. Turn the loin and cook the other side until the breadcrumbs are golden and the pork is just cooked. Place the pan in the oven and cook the pork for a further 5 minutes. Transfer the pork to a wire rack, cover with aluminium foil and leave to rest and cool for 10 minutes.

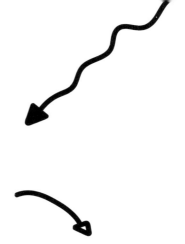

4/ Thinly slice the cabbage using a mandoline or sharp knife. Combine the mayonnaise and brown sauce in a bowl and spread onto the insides of both slices of bread. Place the pork on one slice of bread and top with the cabbage. Place the remaining slice of bread, sauce side down, on top to complete the sandwich. Press gently and then use a sharp knife to cut the sandwich in half.

Egg ± bacon sandwich w̲ home-made brown sauce.

Growing up in the UK, this was my go-to at weekends, and still is whenever I pop back over to visit. You can't go wrong with crispy, salty and chewy bacon smothered with tangy brown sauce, sandwiched between slices of fresh buttered bread – it's next level stuff. I've added an egg because the alchemy of runny yolk, bacon juices and brown sauce is too good to miss, plus I've used some iceberg lettuce for a bit of freshness and crunch. Make your own brown sauce or use store-bought HP; either way, you'll be happy.

Chef's tip
Bread? Whatever you fancy, there are no rules. You might prefer fluffy white sandwich bread, a bun or perhaps a grain sourdough; a baguette also works well.

Makes
1

Prep time
5 minutes

Cook time
12 minutes

4 rashers streaky bacon
1 tablespoon olive oil
1 egg
unsalted butter, at room temperature
2 slices bread
2 iceberg lettuce leaves, shredded
salt flakes
freshly ground black pepper
Darren's brown sauce (page 6)

1/ Preheat the oven to 180°C (350°F). Line a baking tray with baking paper. Lay the bacon on the tray and bake for 10 minutes, or until cooked to your liking. Remove from the oven.

2/ Heat the olive oil in a non-stick frying pan over medium heat. Crack the egg into the pan and fry for a couple of minutes until the white starts to crisp up around the edge and the yolk is just set but still runny. Remove from the heat.

3/ Meanwhile, generously butter both slices of bread and top one slice with the shredded lettuce. Lay a hot fried egg on the lettuce and season the egg with salt and pepper. Put the bacon on top and add a generous dollop of brown sauce. Top with the remaining slice of bread, buttered side down, and press down gently.

Breakfast tacos.

Filled with chorizo, potato, capsicum (bell pepper) and scrambled egg, these are awesome for breakfast on the run. Simply load 'em and wrap 'em, then you're good to go.

<u>Chef's tip</u>
Making your own tortillas is a great skill to have in your repertoire as a cook and you'll quickly gain the reputation of being the person who goes that extra mile. They are pretty simple to make, but you will need to find some masa harina (corn flour) to get that authentic flavour. See page 3 for the recipe for home-made tortillas.

<u>Makes</u>
8

<u>Prep time</u>
15 minutes

<u>Cook time</u>
45 minutes

2 king edward potatoes, peeled and cut into 1 cm (½ in) dice
1 capsicum (bell pepper), seeded and cut into 1 cm (½ in) dice
60 ml (2 fl oz/½ cup) olive oil
salt flakes
freshly ground black pepper
1 fresh chorizo (about 180 g/ 6½ oz)
6 eggs, cracked into a bowl
75 g (2½ oz) sour cream
1 handful fresh coriander (cilantro) leaves, chopped
8 Corn tortillas (page 3) or store bought

1/ Preheat the oven to 180°C (350°F). Cook the potatoes in a saucepan of salted boiling water for 5 minutes to soften. Drain and place on a baking tray with the capsicum pieces. Drizzle the olive oil over the top and season with salt and pepper. Cook in the oven for 25–30 minutes, shaking the tray every 10 minutes or so, until the potato is golden brown and the capsicum is starting to colour.

2/ Cut the casing from the chorizo and crumble the meat into a bowl with your fingers. Heat a non-stick frying pan over medium heat and cook the chorizo crumbs, stirring regularly, for a couple of minutes to release some of the fat. Continue to cook until the edges of the chorizo start to caramelise. Use a slotted spoon to transfer the chorizo to a plate, leaving the chorizo oil in the pan.

3/ Keep the pan on a medium heat and add the eggs. Use a spatula to move the eggs back and forth gently; this is when you start to break down the eggs and mix the yolk into the white. You don't want the eggs to cook too fast; if they are, take the pan off the heat for a few seconds. Keep moving the eggs with the spatula until they start to thicken and look like scrambled eggs. Add the sour cream and season to taste, then stir again before removing the pan from the heat. Stir in the chorizo and coriander.

4/ Spoon some roasted potato and capsicum into a tortilla and then spoon some scrambled egg over the top. Fill all of the tortillas and serve immediately, garnished with coriander leaves if you wish.

Mushroom quesadilla.

Just because you're time poor in the morning, it doesn't mean a quick bowl of cornflakes is your only option. As long as you've got some tortillas to hand or in the freezer, this dish can be cooked in minutes. Once you've eaten something warm, filling and delicious, you will be totally glad you didn't settle for cereal.

Chef's tips

Any seasonal mushrooms will work just fine for this so have a look at what's on offer. Swiss browns work well, as do portobellos, slippery jacks and king mushrooms. To make life a little easier in the morning, I like to precook my mushroom filling the night before.

For the cheese you need something that is going to melt easily: Monterey Jack is great for this, but you could try a cheddar or gruyère.

Makes
2

Prep time
10 minutes

Cook time
20 minutes

60 ml (2 fl oz/½ cup) olive oil
400 g (14 oz) mushrooms, sliced
1 red onion, finely diced
1 celery stalk, thinly sliced
1 jalapeño, halved, seeded and cut into 5 mm (¼ in) dice
1 garlic clove, finely grated with a microplane
15 g (½ oz) unsalted butter
1 teaspoon fresh thyme leaves
salt flakes
freshly ground black pepper
½ lime
1 tablespoon chopped fresh coriander (cilantro) leaves
2 Corn tortillas (page 3) or store bought
300 g (10½ oz) Monterey Jack cheese, grated

1/ Heat the olive oil in a non-stick frying pan over medium heat and cook the mushrooms for 5–8 minutes until caramelised. Remove the mushrooms with a slotted spoon and transfer to a plate.

2/ Put the onion, celery, jalapeño and garlic in the pan. Cook over medium heat for 5 minutes, or until the vegetables soften and become translucent.

3/ Return the mushrooms to the pan along with the butter and thyme. Season with salt and pepper. Cook for a further 2 minutes and then remove from the heat. Squeeze in some lime juice, add the coriander and stir to combine. Transfer the mushroom mixture to a plate.

4/ Wipe the pan dry with paper towel, then place over medium heat. Add a tortilla to the pan and cook for 10 seconds to warm through, then flip it over. Put half of the grated cheese on one half of the tortilla in the pan and spoon half of the mushroom mixture on top. Fold the empty side of the tortilla over the mushrooms and cook for a couple of minutes to melt the cheese and crisp the outside of the tortilla. Gently flip the tortilla to cook the other side. Use a spatula to remove the quesadilla from the pan. Repeat with the remaining tortilla, cheese and mushroom mixture.

Sausage ± egg muffin.

There's so much to love about these – they're simply fun in a bun – and they're just like the ones you get at that fast-food restaurant except made well! You can buy ready-made English muffins if you like, but if you have a bit of time give my recipe a go, as the home-made version will really take things to the next level.

Chef's tip
You'll need a 7.5 cm (3 in) pastry cutter and four 7.5 cm (3 in) egg rings for this recipe.

Makes
4

Prep time
10 minutes (plus 20 minutes chilling)

Cook time
15 minutes

4 pork sausages, 80–100 g
  (2¾–3½ oz) each
2 tablespoons olive oil
canola oil spray
4 eggs
4 English muffins (page 102),
  cut in half horizontally
60 g (2 oz) cheddar cheese,
  grated
4 teaspoons Tomato ketchup
  (page 5)

1/ Cut out four 8 cm (3¼ in) squares of baking paper. Place one square of paper flat on a work surface and put a 7.5 cm (3 in) round pastry cutter in the middle of the paper. Cut off one end of the sausage and squeeze the meat out of the casing into the ring. Use your hands to push the meat down and flatten it. Remove the pastry cutter and place the patty and baking paper on a tray. Repeat with the remaining sausages to make four patties in total. Refrigerate for a minimum of 20 minutes to set.

2/ Heat the olive oil in a non-stick frying pan over medium heat. When the oil is hot, use the edges of the paper to lift the patties and turn them into the pan, discarding the paper. Cook all four patties at the same time for 4 minutes, then flip them over and cook for a further 4 minutes. Transfer the cooked patties to a warm plate.

3/ Place four 7.5 cm (3 in) egg rings into the frying pan over low heat and lightly spray the insides of the rings with oil spray. Crack an egg into each egg ring and cook for about 4 minutes, or until cooked to your liking. Remove the pan from the heat and use a small sharp knife to release the eggs from the rings if needed.

4/ While the eggs are cooking, heat the grill (broiler) and lightly toast the insides of the muffins. Place one-quarter of the grated cheese onto the bottom half of each muffin and grill (broil) until the cheese is bubbling and melted. Transfer the muffin bases to four plates. Place a patty on the cheese, add an egg and top with a teaspoon of tomato ketchup before sandwiching with the top muffin half. Serve immediately and watch out for that egg yolk burst!

ENGLISH MUFFINS

Chef's tip
Make the dough up to the rolling out stage, then cover and store in the fridge overnight, to cook fresh and easily in the morning.

Makes
12

Prep time
20 minutes
(plus 1–1½ hours resting)

Cook time
35 minutes

425 ml (14½ fl oz) full-cream (whole) milk
45 g (1½ oz) unsalted butter
640 g (1 lb 7 oz/4¼ cups) plain (all-purpose) flour
3 teaspoons caster (superfine) sugar
7 g (¼ oz/1 sachet) active dried yeast
1 teaspoon bicarbonate of soda (baking soda)
1 egg
1 teaspoon salt
Canola oil spray
semolina, for dusting

1/ Heat the milk in a saucepan until warm. Let it cool until tepid before using (if the milk is too hot it may kill the yeast). Melt the butter and set aside until cool.

2/ Put the flour, sugar, yeast and bicarbonate of soda in the bowl of a freestanding electric mixer and attach the hook. Mix on low speed for 1 minute before adding the milk and butter. Mix for another minute, then add the egg and salt and mix for 3 minutes until the dough is smooth and elastic. Transfer the dough to a clean bowl, lightly spray with oil and cover with plastic wrap. Leave the dough to prove for 30 minutes in a warm place. Tip the dough out onto a lightly floured work surface and knock back the dough by gently pushing it down with your knuckles. Use a rolling pin or your hands to roll out or flatten the dough to a 2 cm (¾ in) thickness.

3/ Line two large baking trays with baking paper and sprinkle the semolina over the paper.

4/ Using a 7.5 cm (3 in) round pastry cutter, cut out discs from the dough. Reroll the dough and cut out as many as you can. You should be able to get 12 muffins from the dough.

5/ Place the muffins on the baking trays and dust the tops with more semolina, then lightly cover each tray with plastic wrap. Leave to prove in a warm place for 30–60 minutes, or until expanded and puffed.

6/ Preheat the oven to 170°C (340°F). Heat a non-stick frying pan over medium heat. Gently transfer four muffins to the pan and lightly cook them for 3–4 minutes until a light golden crust has formed, then flip them over and cook for a further 2–3 minutes. Transfer the muffins back to the tray and repeat with the remaining muffins. Place the trays in the oven for about 12 minutes to finish cooking, then transfer to a wire rack to cool.

7/ The muffins can also be used for my Mushroom, ham ± eggs benedict (page 44) or for a quick and easy breakfast topped with jam, honey or a fried egg. They also freeze well.

Emma's Tea Spot sausage buttie.

My sister Emma and I were born in the UK but have both travelled for work and life. She has a cute teashop in Baltimore, USA, which she runs with her husband Ben and their children Ava, Quin, Harper and Hannah. The shop has a charming British feel to it, and serves teas and sandwiches. You can have a bacon or sausage buttie with a sauce of your choice, and I know I'm biased but they are awesome! If you ever find yourself in Baltimore, then pop in to Emma's Tea Spot on Harford Road for a buttie and tell them I sent you.

Buttie: noun; northern English – informal. Sandwich of cold bread and hot filling.

Chef's tips
You need thick white bread and a hot filling. Make sure the butter is at room temperature so you don't tear the bread when spreading it with butter.

Variations on this are: bacon buttie (streaky crispy bacon in buttered bread) and chip buttie (hot chips in buttered bread).

Makes
1

Prep time
2 minutes

Cook time
8 minutes

50 ml (1¾ fl oz) light olive oil
2 pork sausages
unsalted butter, at room temperature
2 slices 'doorstop' (extra thick) white bread
2 tablespoons Darren's brown sauce (page 6) and/or Tomato ketchup (page 5)
1 mug of strong English breakfast tea, with milk
1 English newspaper

1/ Heat a non-stick frying pan over medium heat, add the olive oil and sausages and cook for 7–8 minutes, turning frequently, until cooked through. Reserve in the pan while you assemble the buttie.

2/ Spread the butter on both slices of bread. Cut the hot sausages in half horizontally and lay onto one slice of bread. Top with the sauce(s). Sandwich with the remaining slice of bread and cut in half into rectangles, or into four triangles if you think you are posh. Serve with a mug of tea and the newspaper.

Cream cheese, salmon ± caper bagel.

It's not a breakfast book without a bagel, right? I won't give you a recipe for bagels as they are lengthy to make and, to be honest, you can buy good-quality, inexpensive ones these days. You can literally put anything on a bagel, but cream cheese and salmon is a classic combo.

Chef's tip
You won't need all the pickled shallots for this recipe, so store the leftovers in a container in the fridge for next time.

Makes
2

Prep time
10 minutes (plus 30 minutes soaking and standing)

Cook time
5 minutes

Quick pickled shallots
3 French shallots
75 ml (2½ fl oz) white-wine
  vinegar
2 teaspoons caster (superfine)
  sugar
1 teaspoon salt flakes
1 tablespoon fresh dill fronds

2 plain bagels
100 g (3½ oz) cream cheese,
  softened
4 slices smoked salmon
2 teaspoons capers
freshly ground black pepper

1/ For the pickled shallots, peel the shallots and slice thinly using a mandoline or sharp knife. Separate the slices and put them in a bowl of boiling water to soak. Leave for 10 minutes before draining.

2/ Combine the vinegar, sugar and salt in a small saucepan over medium heat, stirring to dissolve the sugar. Remove the pan from the heat and set aside to cool. Pour the cooled vinegar mixture over the shallots. Add the dill and leave to stand for 20 minutes before using.

3/ Cut the bagels in half horizontally and lightly toast the cut sides under a hot grill (broiler).

4/ Spread the cream cheese evenly onto the inside of the four bagel halves. Top the two bottom bagel halves with the smoked salmon, capers and some pickled shallots and dill, and season with pepper. Sandwich with the bagel tops.

Toasted breakfast burrito <u>w</u> scrambled egg ± avocado.

Wraps, rolls, tortillas, sandwiches…I love them all, but when they're toasted, I am in heaven. Perfect for breakfast on the go, these burritos are awesome as a wrap but simply sensational after being toasted in the pan. The filling is totally protected in the tortilla, leaving the scrambled eggs and cheese perfectly creamy and piping hot when you cut through.

Chef's tips
Make sure you cook those scrambled eggs until just done; they'll be briefly cooked a second time during toasting and you don't want to end up with rubbery eggs.

Don't overfill your tortillas; you want to be able to completely close the burrito so everything doesn't spill out when you're crisping it up in the pan.

Makes
4

Prep time
10 minutes

Cook time
15 minutes

2 teaspoons olive oil
6 eggs, cracked into a bowl
80 g (2¾ oz) Monterey Jack cheese, grated (or use cheddar or gruyère)
1 red bird's eye chilli, seeded and thinly sliced
1 jalapeño, halved, seeded and finely chopped
2 tablespoons finely chopped fresh coriander (cilantro) leaves
salt flakes
freshly ground black pepper
4 Corn tortillas (page 3) or store bought (you'll need large 18 cm/7 in ones)
½ avocado, peeled and cut into 1 cm (½ in) dice

1/ Heat the oil in a non-stick frying pan over medium heat, then pour in the eggs. When scrambling eggs you need to control the heat of your pan; it should be hot but not too hot. Instead of turning the heat up and down, you can control the cooking of the eggs by moving the pan back and forth from the stove top. Use a heat-resistant spatula to move the eggs back and forth gently; this is when you start to break down the eggs and mix the yolk into the white. You don't want the eggs to cook too fast; if they are, take the pan off the heat for a few seconds. Keep moving the eggs with the spatula until they start to thicken and look like scrambled eggs.

2/ Add half of the cheese, the chilli, jalapeño and coriander and cook for a further 30 seconds before removing the pan from the heat. Fold once more, then season with salt and pepper and reserve in the pan.

3/ Lay the four tortillas down on a work surface and scatter the remaining cheese equally onto each tortilla. Spoon the scrambled eggs into the centre of each one and top with the diced avocado. Roll the burrito by bringing the top half down and wrapping it around the egg, then tuck in the two sides and roll into a log shape. Repeat with the remaining three tortillas.

4/ Heat a non-stick frying pan over low–medium heat. When the pan is hot, add the four burritos and cook them on four sides (to form a cubed rectangle shape) for 2–3 minutes on each side until crispy and golden brown. Remove from the pan, cut in half and serve immediately.

Bressert.

(YOU SWEET LITTLE THING)

Chocolate canelés.

Canelés are yummy little baked treats originating from Bordeaux in France, traditionally served in the morning. You can find them in cool cafes and awesome bakeries everywhere these days and I absolutely love them, especially with a coffee or hot chocolate. This is my twist on the traditional honey version – these are chocolate flavoured and filled with a silky-smooth chocolate cream.

Chef's tips

You need to start this recipe a day ahead, to give the batter time to rest.

The shape of the mould is what gives the canelé its name. These moulds, usually handmade in copper, were very expensive and hard to find, although are becoming more readily available nowadays. The copper moulds, as well as steel or silicone versions, can be found in kitchenware stores and online.

Traditionally, the moulds were lined with beeswax instead of butter, which gave the pastries their crispy exterior and unique perfume. If you are really serious, do a web search for local apiaries or seek a community urban bee company and ask them if you can buy some beeswax.

Makes
24

Prep time
15 minutes (plus minimum 24 hours resting)

Cook time
50 minutes

450 ml (15 fl oz) full-cream (whole) milk
60 g (2 oz) unsalted butter
1 vanilla bean, split lengthways and seeds scraped
200 g (7 oz) chopped dark chocolate, or melts (buttons)
4 eggs
1 egg yolk
250 g (9 oz/2 cups) icing (confectioners') sugar
100 g (3½ oz/3⅔ cup) plain (all-purpose) flour
capful of rum
finely grated zest of 1 orange
Chocolate cream (page 11)

1/ Heat the milk, butter and vanilla seeds in a saucepan over medium heat until the butter has melted and the milk has just reached boiling point. Remove the pan from the heat, add the chocolate and stir until it has completely melted. Set aside.

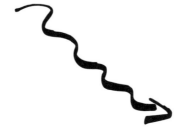

2/ Mix the eggs and egg yolks together in a bowl. Sieve the icing sugar and flour together into another bowl. Add the eggs and stir gently with a fork. Pour the warm chocolate milk into the bowl and mix with a fork or spatula to remove the lumps. Try not to beat too much air into the batter at this stage. Stir in the rum and orange zest. Transfer the batter into a container and store in the fridge for a minimum of 24 hours.

3/ Remove the batter from the fridge and strain it through a sieve into a clean jug or container. Store in the fridge again for up to 1 week or use immediately.

4/ Preheat the oven to 200°C (400°F). Prepare the canelé moulds. You can either line them the traditional way using a beeswax and butter mixture (see right) or brush the moulds with melted butter. If using only butter, chill the moulds in the fridge beforehand so the butter coats the sides more evenly.

5/ Gently stir the batter with a spoon to unsettle the flour, which may have settled to the bottom of the container. Pour the batter into the prepared moulds, filling each one three-quarters full. Place the moulds on a baking tray and bake the canelés for 30 minutes, then turn the tray around and bake for a further 15 minutes until dark brown. Remove from the oven and leave to cool for 10 minutes in the moulds; this ensures the crispy exterior. Set a timer for this, because if you leave them for too long in the moulds, you will run the risk of them sticking.

6/ Turn the canelés out onto a wire rack and leave to cool before piping the chocolate cream onto the top of each one.

BEESWAX IN CANELÉ MOULDS

Prep time
15 minutes

Cook time
5 minutes

24 canelé moulds
150 g (5½ oz) beeswax (see
    Chef's tips, page 112)
150 g (5½ oz) Clarified butter
    (page 4)

1/ Heat the canelé moulds in the preheated 200°C (400°F) oven for 10 minutes.

2/ Place a wire rack over a baking tray. Melt the beeswax in a small saucepan over low heat. Add the clarified butter and mix to combine and warm through.

3/ Pour the mixture into a warmed canelé mould, filling it up to the lip. Holding the mould with tongs or a cloth (or wear an oven glove), pour the mixture back into the saucepan. Turn the mould upside down on the rack to drain. Repeat the process with each mould.

4/ Put the rack and moulds into the fridge to set the coating. Scrape any excess beeswax mixture on the tray back into the pan for reuse or discard it in the bin. Please don't pour any excess beeswax down the sink as it WILL block your drain.

Anytime waffles w̲ bacon ± maple syrup.

Yum! There really is nothing better than fresh home-made fluffy waffles and salty, crunchy bacon drizzled with maple syrup. And, best of all, the waffles are super easy to make if you've got my secret waffle dry mix on hand. Take your breakfast game to new heights.

Chef's tip
The dry mix is enough to make 14 waffles, so make up a batch and store any left-over mix in a sealed container in the fridge so it's ready to go next time.

Makes
4

Prep time
15 minutes (plus 30 minutes proving)

Cook time
10 minutes

Waffle dry mix
700 g (1 lb 9 oz) plain (all-purpose) flour
14 g (½ oz/2 sachets) active dried yeast
2 teaspoons caster (superfine) sugar
1½ teaspoons salt
1 teaspoon bicarbonate of soda (baking soda)

Waffles
200 g (7 oz) Waffle dry mix (see recipe above)
300 ml (10 fl oz) full-cream (whole) milk
60 g (2 oz) unsalted butter
1 egg
canola oil spray

crispy bacon, to serve
maple syrup, to serve

1/ For the waffle dry mix, sieve all of the ingredients into a bowl. Transfer the mix to a plastic container, cover with the lid and store in the fridge.

2/ For the waffles, put 200 g (7 oz) of dry mix in a large bowl and make a well in the centre. This quantity will make four waffles, so save the left-over mix for next time (see Chef's tip).

3/ Heat the milk and butter in a saucepan over medium heat until the butter has melted. Remove from the heat and leave to cool a little, until lukewarm. Crack the egg into the milk and use a fork to lightly beat together.

4/ Trickle the milk mixture into the well in the dry mix, stirring with the fork to eliminate the lumps, to form a smooth, thick batter. Place the batter in a warm spot, such as near a warm oven or on a sunny windowsill, to prove. When the batter has expanded in size it will be ready to use – this probably will take 20–30 minutes.

5/ Heat a waffle iron and grease well with oil spray. Add a quarter of the batter to the waffle iron and cook for 2 minutes, or until light brown and fluffy. Cook the remaining three waffles. Serve with crispy bacon and a generous drizzle of maple syrup.

ANYTIME WAFFLES
W BACON + MAPLE
SYRUP P116

SAUSAGE +
EGG MUFFIN
P101

RED VELVET MUFFINS W WHITE CHOCOLATE P151

BUTTERMILK PANCAKES W LEMON + BLUEBERRIES P120

Buttermilk pancakes <u>w</u> lemon ± blueberries.

Pancakes are a fun start to the day, and something the kids can help you prepare. These pancakes are thick but still light and fluffy, and are made even more luxurious with the addition of crème fraîche into the batter.

Chef's tip
Making the batter the night before not only allows the flavour to develop but also gives the batter time to thicken, resulting in an even thicker, fluffier pancake.

Makes
10

Prep time
10 minutes (plus overnight resting)

Cook time
5 minutes per pancake

180 g (6½ oz) plain (all-purpose) flour
2 teaspoons baking powder
½ teaspoon bicarbonate of soda (baking soda)
2½ tablespoons caster (superfine) sugar
1 teaspoon salt
180 ml (6 fl oz) buttermilk
3 eggs, lightly beaten
100 g (3½ oz) crème fraîche, at room temperature
50 g (1¾ oz) unsalted butter, melted and cooled
finely grated zest of 1 lemon
canola oil spray
250 g (9 oz) blueberries
Lemon curd (see right), to serve
extra crème fraîche and blueberries, to serve

1/ Sieve the flour, baking powder and bicarbonate of soda into a bowl and add the sugar and salt. Slowly mix in the buttermilk and then the eggs, adding them a little at a time. Add the crème fraîche and the cooled melted butter and stir to combine. Pass the mixture through a sieve into a container and then add the lemon zest. Cover and rest the batter in the fridge overnight.

2/ Spray a non-stick frying pan with oil spray and place the pan over low–medium heat. To test if your pan is hot enough to cook the pancakes, flick a tiny bit of water onto the pan. If it's ready, the water will sizzle immediately.

3/ Take a small ladle or large spoon of batter and pour it into the centre of the pan, using the back of the ladle to spread the pancake out to an even round. Dot the pancake with ten or so blueberries and cook for about 3 minutes, or until bubbles start to appear and break in the middle of the pancake. Flip the pancake over and cook for a further 1–2 minutes until the middle springs back when pushed with a finger. Remove to a wire rack and repeat the process to cook all the batter.

4/ Serve the pancakes warm with the lemon curd, a dollop of crème fraîche and extra blueberries.

LEMON CURD

Makes
600 g (1 lb 5 oz)

Prep time
10 minutes

Cook time
10 minutes

4 g (¼ oz/2 sheets) gold-strength gelatine leaves
4 eggs
finely grated zest and juice of 3 lemons
130 g (4½ oz) unsalted butter, at room temperature
200 g (7 oz) caster (superfine) sugar

1/ Soak the gelatine leaves in a bowl of cold water for 2 minutes to soften. Drain the gelatine and gently squeeze out the excess water.

2/ Put the eggs, lemon zest and juice, butter and sugar in a heatproof bowl and mix with a whisk to combine well. Place the bowl over a saucepan of gently simmering water, ensuring the base of the bowl isn't touching the water. Whisk the mixture constantly until the curd has reached a temperature of 82°C (180°F); use a digital thermometer to accurately check the temperature.

3/ Remove the bowl from the heat and whisk in the gelatine, mixing well until the gelatine has dissolved, then pour the curd through a sieve into a bowl. Set this bowl into a larger bowl of iced water and stir regularly to cool the curd down quickly. Spoon the curd into a container and store in the fridge for up to 4 days.

Chocolate streusel brioche.

You don't have to be a master baker or get up at 3 am to make something exceptional for a baked breakfast. With a bit of planning and some preparation you can still have that lie-in, plus have a delicious buttery brioche bun that tastes as good as the ones from that trendy bakery down the road.

Chef's tips

Start this recipe the day before and partially prove the dough before resting it in the fridge for a few hours. Before bed, weigh out your dough portions and roll them into balls, then place them into the moulds, leave to prove again and then chill overnight. The next morning, take the dough out of the fridge and let it prove again before baking.

You can make the chocolate streusel ahead of time if you like and store it in a sealed container in the fridge.

Makes
6

Prep time
40 minutes (plus resting, proving overnight and on the day)

Cook time
20 minutes

190 g (6½ oz) strong (baker's) flour
20 g (¾ oz) caster (superfine) sugar
5 g (¼ oz) active dried yeast
2 eggs
1 egg yolk
pinch of salt
95 g (3¼ oz) unsalted butter, chilled and diced
canola oil spray
250 g (9 oz) Chocolate cream (page 11)

Chocolate streusel
50 g (1¾ oz) unsalted butter, at room temperature
50 g (1¾ oz) soft brown sugar
40 g (1½ oz) plain (all-purpose) flour
40 g (1½ oz) ground almonds
40 g (1½ oz) Dutch (unsweetened) cocoa powder

Egg wash
1 egg yolk
3 tablespoons thickened (whipping) cream

1/ Put the flour, sugar, yeast, eggs and egg yolk in the bowl of a freestanding electric mixer and attach the dough hook. Knead on low speed for 10 minutes before adding the salt. Mix again for a further 5 minutes.

2/ Turn the machine to medium speed and add the butter, one cube at a time, ensuring it is mixed in well before adding the next cube. Once all of the butter has been added, the dough should be smooth, shiny and elastic.

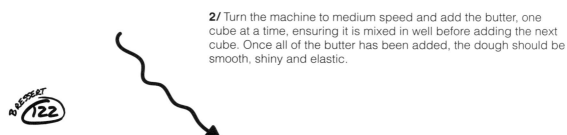

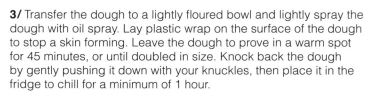

3/ Transfer the dough to a lightly floured bowl and lightly spray the dough with oil spray. Lay plastic wrap on the surface of the dough to stop a skin forming. Leave the dough to prove in a warm spot for 45 minutes, or until doubled in size. Knock back the dough by gently pushing it down with your knuckles, then place it in the fridge to chill for a minimum of 1 hour.

4/ Remove the dough from the fridge and turn it out onto a lightly floured work surface. Weigh out 70 g (2½ oz) portions of dough (you should have six portions). Any remaining dough can be evenly distributed among the other portions.

5/ Spray six holes of a 12-hole standard muffin tin or grease six aluminium cups with oil spray. Roll the portions of dough into balls and place into each hole or cup. Spray the surface of each brioche with oil spray and lay a piece of plastic wrap over the top. Ensure the plastic is not wrapped tightly around the brioche but just resting on top, to allow enough space for the dough to prove. Place in a warm spot to prove for 30 minutes, then transfer to the fridge to slow prove overnight.

6/ The next day, remove the dough from the fridge and place in a warm spot to prove for about 45 minutes, or until it has risen and doubled in size. Gently remove the plastic wrap.

7/ While the dough is proving, make the chocolate streusel. Preheat the oven to 170°C (340°F) and line a baking tray with baking paper. Put all of the streusel ingredients in a bowl and use your fingers to combine everything together, to create a sandy texture with no butter lumps. Scatter the chocolate crumb evenly onto the lined tray. Cook for 8–10 minutes until lightly baked and then remove from the oven and set aside to cool.

8/ Increase the oven temperature to 180°C (350°F). For the egg wash, combine the egg yolk and cream together. Using a pastry brush, gently brush the egg wash over the surface of each brioche, then sprinkle a tablespoon of chocolate streusel onto each bun. Bake for 10 minutes until golden brown, then remove from the oven and leave to cool for 3 minutes. Remove the brioche from the moulds and place on a wire rack to cool.

9/ Transfer the chocolate cream into a piping (icing) bag fitted with a small plain nozzle. Take a small knife and make a hole in the base of each brioche. Pipe the chocolate cream into the brioche, filling it with as much cream as you can without splitting the bun. Serve immediately.

Strawberry cheesecake brioche.

I know! You're trying this recipe after the amazing success of the Chocolate streusel brioche on the previous page. It's given you massive confidence. Awesome news! Now it's time to take it to the next level and leave your family wondering if you've secretly been going to baking school.

Chef's tip
We are using a basic brioche dough recipe here and cutting it in two. You're going to colour one half of the dough red, sit it on top of the uncoloured half, then do some fancy rolling and scrolling to create an amazing two-toned scroll effect. You'll be grinning from ear to ear with pride.

Makes
6

Prep time
40 minutes (plus resting, proving overnight and on the day)

Cook time
10 minutes

190 g (6½ oz) strong (baker's) flour
20 g (¾ oz) caster (superfine) sugar
5 g (¼ oz) active dried yeast
2 eggs
1 egg yolk
pinch of salt
95 g (3¼ oz) unsalted butter, chilled and diced
canola oil spray
red food colouring, as needed
120 g (4½ oz) Strawberry jam (page 10)
Cream cheese frosting (page 11)

Egg wash
1 egg yolk
3 tablespoons thickened (whipping) cream

1/ Put the flour, sugar, yeast, eggs and egg yolk in the bowl of a freestanding electric mixer and attach the dough hook. Knead on low speed for 10 minutes before adding the salt. Mix again for a further 5 minutes.

2/ Turn the machine to medium speed and add the butter, one cube at a time, ensuring it is mixed in well before adding the next cube. Once all of the butter has been added, the dough should be smooth, shiny and elastic.

3/ Remove the dough from the machine and divide it in half (weigh the dough on kitchen scales for accuracy). Transfer one portion of dough to a lightly floured bowl and lightly spray with oil spray. Lay plastic wrap on the surface of the dough to stop a skin forming.

4/ Return the remaining dough portion to the mixer bowl and place back onto the machine. Turn the machine to medium speed and add enough red food colouring to colour the dough a bright strawberry red. Transfer to a lightly floured bowl; lightly spray the dough with oil spray. Lay plastic wrap on the surface of the dough.

5/ Leave both doughs to prove in a warm spot for 45 minutes, or until doubled in size. Knock back the doughs by gently pushing them down with your knuckles, then place them in the fridge to chill for a minimum of 1 hour.

6/ Remove the doughs from the fridge. Turn the uncoloured dough out onto a lightly floured work surface. Using a rolling pin and more flour if needed, roll out the dough to a 10 cm x 5 cm (4 in x 2 in) rectangle, with a 1 cm (½ in) thickness. Repeat with the red dough, ensuring it is roughly the same dimensions. Place the red dough on top of the uncoloured dough and press down gently. Using the rolling pin and a little more flour, roll out the two doughs together to form a 25 cm x 8 cm (10 in x 3¼ in) rectangle.

7/ For the egg wash, combine the egg yolk and cream together. Roll the dough into a scroll by rolling the longer length upwards to the top length. Use a pastry brush to brush a little of the egg wash along the top length of the dough, to help stick the scroll together. You should be left with a roll of dough approximately 25 cm (10 in) in length. Use a knife to cut the scroll into six even pieces. Refrigerate the remaining egg wash for later use.

8/ Spray six holes of a 12-hole standard muffin tin or grease six aluminium cups with oil spray. Lay each scroll, cut side up, into each hole or cup. Spray the surface of the scrolls with oil spray and lay a piece of plastic wrap over the top. Ensure the plastic is not wrapped tightly around the brioche but just resting on top, to allow enough space for the dough to prove. Place in a warm spot to prove for 30 minutes, then transfer to the fridge to slow prove overnight.

9/ The next day, remove the brioche from the fridge and place in a warm spot to prove for about 45 minutes, or until they have risen and doubled in size.

10/ Preheat the oven to 180°C (350°F). Gently remove the plastic wrap and then carefully brush the egg wash onto the surface of each brioche. Bake for 10 minutes until golden brown, then remove from the oven and leave to cool for 3 minutes. Remove the brioche from the moulds and place on a wire rack to cool.

11/ Transfer the strawberry jam into a piping (icing) bag fitted with a small plain nozzle. Take a small knife and make a hole in the base of each brioche. Pipe the jam into the brioche, filling it with as much jam as you can without splitting the bun. Transfer the cream cheese frosting into a piping bag and pipe a large bulb on the top of each scroll.

Chocolate ± vanilla glazed doughnuts.

The breakfast of champions! If you're gonna have a cheat day, you may as well do it properly.

<u>**Chef's tips**</u>
You'll need to deep-fry these, so that means you need to be careful with large pans of hot oil.

I have filled my doughnuts with a silky-smooth white chocolate and vanilla cream but you could use jam, Lemon curd (page 121) or Chocolate cream (page 11).

<u>**Makes**</u>
10

<u>**Prep time**</u>
30 minutes (plus 1½ hours or overnight proving)

<u>**Cook time**</u>
5 minutes for glaze plus 6–8 minutes per doughnut

Doughnuts
250 g (9 oz/1⅔ cups) plain (all-purpose) flour
100 g (3½ oz) unsalted butter, at room temperature
3 eggs
5 g (¼ oz) active dried yeast
2 teaspoons caster (superfine) sugar
50 ml (1¾ fl oz) full-cream (whole) milk
½ teaspoon salt
canola oil spray
1 litre (34 fl oz/4 cups) canola or sunflower oil, for frying
300 g (10½ oz) White chocolate ± vanilla cream (page 10)

Glaze
10 g (¼ oz/5 sheets) gold-strength gelatine leaves
180 g (6½ oz) caster (superfine) sugar
60 g (2 oz/½ cup) Dutch (unsweetened) cocoa powder
140 ml (4½ fl oz) water
100 ml (3½ fl oz) thickened (whipping) cream

1/ For the doughnuts, put the flour, butter, eggs, yeast, sugar and milk in the bowl of a freestanding electric mixer and attach the dough hook. Knead on low speed for 8 minutes. Add the salt, then increase the speed to medium and mix for a further 5 minutes.

2/ Transfer the dough to a lightly floured bowl, cover with a damp tea towel (dish towel) and leave the dough to prove in a warm place for up to 1 hour, or until it has doubled in size. Turn the dough out onto a lightly floured work surface and knock back the dough by gently pushing it down with your knuckles.

3/ Cut out ten 5 cm (2 in) square pieces of baking paper. Using lightly floured hands, weigh out 50–55 g (1¾–2 oz) portions of dough (you should have ten portions). Shape the dough into balls and place each one on a piece of baking paper. Transfer to a baking tray and lightly spray the surface of each ball with oil spray. Lay plastic wrap over the top to stop a skin forming. You can now refrigerate these overnight for the next morning, or continue. If refrigerating overnight, remove the dough balls from the fridge 1 hour before cooking to give them time to prove sufficiently. Otherwise, leave them to prove in a warm place for 30 minutes, or until they have nearly doubled in size.

4/ While the doughnuts are proving, prepare the glaze. Soak the gelatine leaves in a bowl of cold water for 2 minutes to soften. Drain the gelatine and gently squeeze out the excess water.

5/ Put the sugar and cocoa powder in a large bowl and stir in the water and then the cream to make a lump-free paste. Transfer the paste to a saucepan and place over medium heat. Bring the mixture to the boil for 1 minute, stirring constantly with a spatula to prevent sticking. Remove from the heat, stir in the gelatine until dissolved, then pour the glaze through a sieve into a shallow bowl. Leave to cool at room temperature.

6/ When the doughnuts have proved, half-fill a large saucepan with the oil and heat to 170°C (340°F); use a digital thermometer to accurately check the temperature. Cook the doughnuts one at a time by picking up the edges of the baking paper and gently dropping the whole thing into the hot oil. The paper will release from the doughnut and you can remove this from the oil using tongs. Cook the doughnut for 3–4 minutes on each side, using a slotted metal spoon to flip it over. Lift out with the spoon and place on paper towel to drain. Repeat until all the doughnuts are cooked and leave them to cool.

7/ Use a small knife to make an incision in the base of each doughnut. Transfer the chocolate and vanilla cream into a piping (icing) bag fitted with a small plain nozzle. Pipe the cream into the hole – about 30 g (1 oz) of cream per doughnut should be plenty.

8/ Next, glaze the doughnuts. Stir the glaze. If it has cooled sufficiently it will appear thick and shiny; if the glaze is still too hot, then wait until it thickens and is ready to use. Take a filled doughnut and dip the surface into the glaze, then hold the doughnut upside down and gently shake it to remove any drips and excess glaze. Turn the doughnut right side up and place on a serving plate. Repeat with all of the doughnuts. Serve to friends or family and see how popular you've become.

Coconut, quinoa ± white chocolate chip cookies.

Who says you shouldn't eat cookies for breakfast? These are packed with flavour and will give you a sugary energy boost. Plus they've got quinoa in them, so they gotta be good for you…right?

<u>Chef's tip</u>
Scale this recipe up by doubling, tripling or more, then make lots of cookie dough balls and store them in the freezer. You can then bake them as and when you need a cookie hit.

<u>Makes</u>
8

<u>Prep time</u>
15 minutes

<u>Cook time</u>
18 minutes per batch

90 g (3 oz) unsalted butter, at room temperature
30 g (1 oz) light brown sugar
50 g (1¾ oz) dark brown (muscovado) sugar
70 g (2½ oz) caster (superfine) sugar
1 teaspoon salt
½ teaspoon bicarbonate of soda (baking soda), sieved
1 egg
130 g (4½ oz) plain (all-purpose) flour, sieved
60 g (2 oz) puffed quinoa
150 g (5½ oz) white chocolate, roughly chopped
50 g (1¾ oz) flaked coconut
20 g (½ oz) desiccated coconut
finely grated zest of 1 orange

1/ Put the butter, three sugars, salt and bicarbonate of soda in the bowl of a freestanding electric mixer and attach the paddle. Cream on low speed for 1 minute, then use a spatula to scrape down the inside of the bowl to ensure everything has evenly mixed. Increase the speed to medium and beat until pale and smooth.

2/ Add the egg and continue to beat, then add the flour, quinoa, chocolate, flaked and desiccated coconut and orange zest. Beat briefly until all the ingredients are mixed well. Tip out onto a lightly floured work surface and divide the dough into eight equal pieces. Roll each piece of dough into a ball.

3/ Preheat the oven to 180°C (350°F). Line two baking trays with baking paper. Arrange four dough balls on each tray, spacing them evenly apart. Bake the cookies, one tray at a time, on the centre rack of the oven for 16–18 minutes. Remove the tray from the oven and leave to sit for 1 minute before gently pressing each cookie down with a weight, such as the base of a saucepan. Do not squash them completely, just flatten them a little – this will make the cookies crunchy on the outside and chewy in the middle when cooled. Transfer to a wire rack to cool.

Ruby chocolate chip cookies w̲ raspberries ± yoghurt.

Ruby chocolate is the new big thing in chocolate and pastry – it's been called the fourth chocolate after white, dark and milk. The chocolate is made from unfermented cocoa beans, which are naturally pinkish in colour (it's the fermentation process that turns the beans brown), and has a slightly sweet, fruity yet sour flavour, which pairs beautifully with fresh berries and yoghurt. You may have seen those cool ruby-chocolate KitKats, loved in Asian countries…well, here's my offering. Who doesn't want to eat chocolate cookies in the morning, especially when they're pretty in pink!

Chef's tips
Ruby chocolate is new and therefore may be hard to find. It's available online or look for it in specialist ingredient stores.

Buy yoghurt powder from health food stores or online. It's great for adding a yoghurt flavour to cookies, muffins or sponges without adding the wetness of actual yoghurt.

Makes
18

Prep time
15 minutes (plus 30 minutes chilling)

Cook time
17 minutes per batch

220 g (7 oz) unsalted butter
200 g (7 oz) soft brown sugar
180 g (6½ oz) caster (superfine) sugar
2 teaspoons salt
1 teaspoon bicarbonate of soda (baking soda), sieved
1 vanilla bean, split lengthways and seeds scraped
2 eggs, whole
400 g (14 oz/2⅔ cups) plain (all-purpose) flour, sieved
100 g (3½ oz) yoghurt powder, sieved
200 g (7 oz) white chocolate melts (buttons)
300 g (10½ oz) ruby chocolate melts (buttons)
Greek-style yoghurt, to serve
100 g (3½ oz) raspberries, to serve

1/ Put the butter, brown sugar, caster sugar, salt, bicarbonate of soda and vanilla seeds in the bowl of a freestanding electric mixer and attach the paddle. Cream on low–medium speed for about 8 minutes until pale and smooth, using a spatula to scrape down the inside of the bowl to ensure everything has evenly mixed.

2/ Add the eggs, one at a time, beating continuously, and again scraping down the inside of the bowl. Add the flour, yoghurt powder, 150 g (5½ oz) of the white chocolate and 250 g (9 oz) of the ruby chocolate and beat on low speed until incorporated.

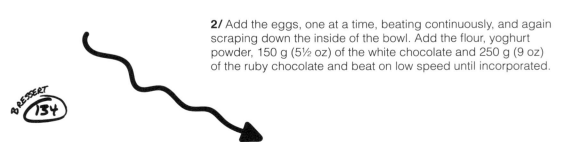

3/ Remove the dough from the machine. Use lightly floured hands and kitchen scales to weigh out 75 g (2¾ oz) portions of dough (you should have about 18 portions). Any remaining dough can be evenly distributed among the other portions of dough. Roll the dough into balls, place on a tray and refrigerate for a minimum of 30 minutes.

4/ Preheat the oven to 180°C (350°F). Line a baking tray with baking paper. Transfer half the chilled dough balls onto the tray. Bake for 17 minutes, then remove the tray from the oven and leave to sit for 1 minute before gently pressing each cookie down with a weight, such as the base of a saucepan. Do not squash them completely, just flatten them a little – this will make the cookies crunchy on the outside and chewy in the middle when cooled.

5/ Dot half the remaining white chocolate and ruby chocolate onto the surface of the warm cookies. Return the tray to the oven for about 30 seconds to 'shine' the chocolate – no longer than this or the buttons will start to melt and lose their shape.

6/ Remove from the oven and cool on the tray for 2 minutes before using a metal spatula or palette knife to lift the cookies onto a wire rack. Repeat for the second batch of cookies. Serve with yoghurt and raspberries.

Chocolate ± orange marmalade grilled croissant.

This flavour combo reminds me of Jaffa cakes from my childhood. Chocolate and orange go really well together, and the tang of the marmalade with the bitter chocolate mean this is not too sweet. The chocolate strips give a fantastic, almost liquid chocolate centre to the croissant.

Chef's tip
Day-old croissants work best for these as they are dry and bake really well.

Makes
2

Prep time
5 minutes

Cook time
12 minutes

50 ml (1¾ fl oz) water
50 g (1¾ oz) caster (superfine) sugar
½ orange, for zesting
2 croissants, preferably day-old
2 tablespoons Classic Seville orange marmalade (page 9)
2 frozen strips Chocolate ± orange filling (page 138)
icing (confectioners') sugar, for dusting

1/ Bring the water and sugar to the boil in a small saucepan over medium heat, stirring until the sugar has dissolved. Remove the pan from the heat, then use a microplane to finely grate the orange zest into the sugar syrup.

2/ Use a serrated knife to cut both croissants lengthways, and open them up. Use a pastry brush to dab some of the sugar syrup onto the cut inside halves of each croissant. Spread the marmalade evenly onto the bottom half of the croissants, top with a frozen chocolate and orange strip and then close the croissants.

3/ Liberally dust the croissants with icing sugar. Preheat a cast-iron grill pan (I used one that has a lid) over high heat. Add the croissants and press down with the hot lid. Cook for 8–10 minutes until the croissants are toasted and have grill marks, and the filling has melted. Alternatively, use a sandwich press to cook them.

CHOCOLATE + ORANGE FILLING

Makes
16 strips

Prep time
10 minutes (plus 2 hours freezing)

Cook time
5 minutes

250 ml (8½ fl oz/1 cup) thickened (whipping) cream
20 g (¾ oz) liquid glucose
275 g (9½ oz) dark chocolate, chopped
50 g (1¾ oz) unsalted butter, at room temperature
1 orange, for zesting
capful of orange liqueur such as Grand Marnier or Cointreau (optional)
canola oil spray

1/ Put the cream and glucose in a small saucepan over medium heat and bring to a gentle simmer.

2/ Put the chocolate and butter in a tall, narrow measuring jug and pour in the hot cream. Use a microplane to finely grate in the orange zest, then add the orange liqueur, if using. Leave the mixture to sit for 30 seconds, then blend to a smooth cream using a hand-held blender.

3/ Lightly spray a shallow 25 cm x 15 cm (10 in x 6 in) tray with oil spray, then line with plastic wrap, leaving the plastic overhanging the sides. Use your hands to smooth the plastic so there are no wrinkles. Pour the chocolate mixture into the tray, then place in the freezer for a minimum of 2 hours until set hard.

4/ Lift the set chocolate cream out of the tray, then remove and discard the plastic. Place the chocolate on a chopping board and use a large knife to cut the slab in half lengthways – you will end up with two slabs measuring 25 cm x 7.5 cm (10 in x 3 in). Cut each half into eight 3 cm (1¼ in) wide strips to give you 16 strips, 3 cm x 7.5 cm (1¼ in x 3 in). Discard any trim, put the strips back onto the tray and return to the freezer until needed. Store the left-over strips in a container in the freezer for next time.

ALMOND, PEAR
+ CHOCOLATE
CROISSANT P140

CHOCOLATE + ORANGE
MARMALADE GRILLED
CROISSANT
P137

Almond, pear ± chocolate croissant.

As a general rule, whenever we buy croissants in our house we usually don't have any left over. I can easily scoff a fistful, so I am encouraged by my wife to buy only one croissant per person instead of fifteen. If we did have a couple kicking around, though, this might be something I would use them up for.

Chef's tip
Pear works well with almond and chocolate, we all know that, but they can be crunchy sometimes so try to choose a beautiful ripe one that doesn't need cooking beforehand. I used soft, ripe Victorian honey pears and they were just delicious, and not at all crunchy in the pastry.

Makes
4

Prep time
15 minutes

Cook time
18 minutes

125 g (4½ oz) unsalted butter, at room temperature
125 g (4½ oz/1 cup) icing (confectioners') sugar
pinch of salt
½ vanilla bean, split lengthways and seeds scraped
1 egg
1 egg yolk
125 g (4½ oz/1¼ cups) ground almonds
capful of rum
75 ml (2¾ fl oz) water
75 g (2¾ oz) caster (superfine) sugar
½ lemon, for zesting
1 ripe pear, peeled and quartered with the core removed
4 croissants, preferably day-old
60 g (2 oz) dark chocolate melts (buttons)
100 g (3½ oz) flaked almonds

1/ Put the butter, icing sugar, salt and vanilla seeds in the bowl of a freestanding electric mixer and attach the paddle. Cream on low speed for 2 minutes, then use a spatula to scrape down the inside of the bowl to ensure everything has evenly mixed. Continue to beat for about 6 minutes, or until the mixture is smooth and pale. Scrape down the bowl with a spatula again and continue to beat if needed.

2/ Beat in the egg followed by the egg yolk. Scrape down the inside of the bowl and continue to mix. Add the ground almonds and mix for a further 2 minutes before adding the rum. Remove the bowl from the machine.

3/ Bring the water and sugar to the boil in a small saucepan over medium heat, stirring until the sugar has dissolved. Use a microplane to finely grate the lemon zest into the sugar syrup.

4/ Preheat the oven to 180°C (350°F). Line a baking tray or sheet with baking paper. Slice the pear quarters into thin slices (you will use one pear quarter for each croissant).

5/ Use a serrated knife to cut each croissant lengthways, and open them up. Use a pastry brush to dab some of the sugar syrup onto the cut inside halves of each croissant. Reserve 4 teaspoons of the almond mixture and then use a spoon or knife to spread the remaining mixture evenly onto the bottom half of each croissant. Scatter about 15 g (½ oz) of the chocolate on top of the almond mix, then arrange the pear slices on top. Close the croissants and brush the remaining syrup over them before smudging a teaspoon of the reserved almond mix onto the top of each one.

6/ Place the croissants on the baking tray and scatter some flaked almonds on top. Bake for 16 minutes, then remove from the oven and leave to sit for 1 minute before serving.

Fruit ± nut breakfast bars.

These are dead easy to make, so whip up stacks for those days when you just gotta run. The fruit and nuts will give you energy for hours and the honey makes it all taste delicious.

Chef's tip

Invent your own breakfast bars and use whatever dried fruit, seeds or nuts you fancy. The main thing is to keep the total quantity of dry ingredients similar to the weights listed in the recipe.

Makes

20

Prep time

**15 minutes
(plus 2 hours setting)**

Cook time

5 minutes

canola oil spray
200 g (7 oz) honey
25 g (1 oz) puffed quinoa
25 g (1 oz) puffed rice
25 g (1 oz) cacao nibs
50 g (1¾ oz) pistachio nuts
75 g (2¾ oz/¾ cup) walnuts, roughly chopped
75 g (2¾ oz/½ cup) almonds, lightly toasted and roughly chopped
40 g (1½ oz/¼ cup) cashew nuts
25 g (1 oz) pepitas (pumpkin seeds)
25 g (1 oz) sunflower seeds
50 g (1¾ oz) dried cranberries
¼ teaspoon ground cinnamon
¼ teaspoon ground ginger
finely grated zest of ½ orange
½ tablespoon sesame seeds, toasted
½ teaspoon salt flakes

1/ Lightly spray a non-stick 30 cm x 20 cm (12 in x 8 in) shallow baking tray with oil spray.

2/ Put the honey in a saucepan. Put all the remaining ingredients in a large heatproof bowl. Heat the honey over medium heat to 140°C (284°F); use a digital thermometer to accurately check the temperature. Remove the pan from the heat.

3/ Pour the hot honey onto the ingredients in the bowl, taking care as the honey tends to spit at this temperature. Quickly combine everything using a silicone spatula. Transfer the mixture to the tray, pressing it hard into the corners, and level it off with the spatula. Leave to cool at room temperature for a minimum of 2 hours to set.

4/ Remove from the tray and transfer to a chopping board. Use a large sharp knife (oiled if necessary) to cut the slab into 3 cm x 10 cm (1¼ in x 4 in) bars. Store the bars in a sealed container in the pantry.

Hot cross buns.

These are a real favourite of mine, and thankfully they're only around once a year because any more would be dangerous! I have mine untoasted, straight out of the oven, with loads of butter. It's such a nice change to make your own rather than buying them. And it makes you feel less guilty as you spread half a block of butter on your fourth bun. Jubbly.

Chef's tip
Do the hard stuff the day before and let the buns slow prove overnight for better flavour and ease the next day.

Makes
8

Prep time
20 minutes (plus resting, proving overnight and on the day)

Cook time
15 minutes

Starter
240 ml (8 fl oz) water
28 g (1 oz/4 sachets) active dried yeast
80 g (2¾ oz) strong (baker's) flour
2 teaspoons caster (superfine) sugar
3 teaspoons skim milk powder

Buns
30 g (1 oz) currants
30 g (1 oz) sultanas (golden raisins), chopped
30 g (1 oz) mixed peel (mixed candied citrus peel), chopped
400 g (14 oz) strong (baker's) flour
80 g (2¾ oz) caster (superfine) sugar
85 g (3 oz) unsalted butter
1 egg
1 teaspoon salt
½ teaspoon ground cinnamon
½ teaspoon freshly grated nutmeg
½ teaspoon ground cloves
finely grated zest of 1 lemon
canola oil spray

Egg wash
2 egg yolks
1 tablespoon milk
pinch of salt

Cross
75 g (2¾ oz) plain (all-purpose) flour
50 g (1¾ oz) caster (superfine) sugar
40 ml (1¼ fl oz) water

Syrup
100 ml (3½ fl oz) water
100 g (3½ oz) caster (superfine) sugar

1/ For the starter, combine all the ingredients in a bowl and whisk together. Cover with plastic wrap and leave in a warm place for up to 45 minutes, or until doubled in size.

2/ For the buns, put the currants, sultanas and mixed peel in a bowl. Cover with hot water and leave to soak for 10 minutes, then drain.

3/ Put the flour, sugar, butter, egg, salt and spices in the bowl of a freestanding electric mixer and attach the hook. Mix on low speed for 2 minutes, then add the starter. Increase the speed to medium and mix for a further 5–6 minutes.

4/ Turn the speed back to low, then add the drained soaked fruit and lemon zest and mix for 1 minute. Remove the dough from the mixing bowl and transfer it to a lightly floured bowl. Lightly spray the surface of the dough with oil spray, lay plastic wrap over the top and leave it to prove in a warm place for 30 minutes, or until doubled in size.

5/ Once doubled, remove the dough from the bowl and place on a lightly floured work surface. Knock back the dough by gently pushing it down with your knuckles. Cover with plastic wrap and leave to rest for 10 minutes.

6/ Use kitchen scales to weigh out eight equal portions of dough. Roll each portion into a ball and place on a greased baking tray, spacing them apart. Lightly spray each ball with oil spray and lay a piece of plastic wrap over the top. Ensure the plastic is not wrapped tightly around the buns but just resting on top, to allow enough space for the buns to expand and prove. Place the tray in the fridge to slow prove overnight.

7/ The next day, remove the tray from the fridge and place it in a warm place for the dough to prove for about 30 minutes, or until the buns have almost doubled in size.

8/ While the buns are proving, prepare the other elements. For the egg wash, combine the egg yolks, milk and salt in a small bowl. For the cross, whisk the flour, sugar and water together until smooth; transfer this to a piping (icing) bag fitted with a small plain nozzle. For the sugar syrup, bring the water and sugar to the boil in a saucepan over medium heat, stirring until the sugar has dissolved. Preheat the oven to 180°C (350°F).

9/ Gently remove the plastic wrap from the buns and use a pastry brush to lightly brush the egg wash onto the surface of each bun, ensuring the dough does not accidentally get knocked back by heavy-handedness. Pipe the crosses on top of the buns.

10/ Bake the buns for 12–14 minutes, then remove the tray from the oven. Brush the sugar syrup over the top of each bun, transfer to a wire rack and leave to cool.

Chocolate, yoghurt ± lemon cornflake tarts.

Now we're cooking! These awesome chocolate, tangy tarts may not be a conventional breakfast but they'll give you that burst of energy you're going to need for the big day ahead. With lots of components and textures, these will make you look like a complete pro when you bring them to the table. Don't try to make everything on the day, though, or you'll be serving these for late lunch rather than breakfast.

Chef's tip
Plan ahead of time for minimum stress. Make the tart cases the day before and store them in a sealed container. The lemon yoghurt and chocolate cream can easily be made on the day, though if you do make them ahead, cover and refrigerate until needed.

Makes
12

Prep time
15 minutes (plus 40 minutes chilling)

Cook time
5 minutes

12 Chocolate tart cases (page 150)
Dutch (unsweetened) cocoa powder, for dusting

Lemon yoghurt
1 lemon, for zesting
300 g (10½ oz) Greek-style yoghurt

Chocolate cream w cornflakes
185 ml (6 fl oz/¾ cup) thickened (whipping) cream
20 g (¾ oz) liquid glucose
170 g (6 oz) dark chocolate, chopped
65 g (2¼ oz) unsalted butter, at room temperature
100 g (3½ oz) cornflakes

1/ Place the prepared tart cases on a tray and set aside.

2/ For the lemon yoghurt, use a microplane to finely grate the lemon zest into the yoghurt. Mix with a spoon to combine. Transfer the lemon yoghurt to a piping (icing) bag (or use a teaspoon) and half fill each tart case (use about 25 g/1 oz per tart). Place the tarts in the freezer for 20 minutes.

3/ Meanwhile, make the chocolate cream. Put the cream and glucose in a small saucepan over medium heat and bring to a gentle simmer. Put the chocolate and butter in a tall, narrow measuring jug and pour in the hot cream. Leave the mixture to sit for 30 seconds, then blend to a smooth cream using a hand-held blender. Stir in the cornflakes and use immediately.

4/ Remove the tray of yoghurt-filled tarts from the freezer. Spoon the chocolate and cornflake mixture into each tart; don't try to neaten the mixture, leave it rough and textured in appearance. Refrigerate for 20 minutes to set. Before serving, dust each tart with cocoa powder.

CHOCOLATE TART CASES

Makes
12

Prep time
20 minutes (plus
50 minutes resting)

Cook time
25 minutes

250 g (9 oz/1⅔ cups) plain
   (all-purpose) flour
30 g (1 oz/¼ cup) Dutch
   (unsweetened) cocoa
   powder
90 g (3 oz/¾ cup) icing
   (confectioners') sugar
pinch of salt
135 g (5 oz) unsalted butter,
   chilled and diced
1 egg
1 egg yolk
canola oil spray
100 g (3½ oz) chopped
   dark chocolate

1/ Put the flour, cocoa powder, icing sugar and salt in the bowl of a freestanding electric mixer and attach the paddle. Turn the machine to low and add the butter, then mix until you have a fine sandy mix. Add the egg and egg yolk and mix again until the dough starts to come together.

2/ Turn the dough out onto a lightly floured work surface and bring it together with your hands to form a ball. Push the ball down to flatten slightly, cover in plastic wrap and refrigerate for 30 minutes.

3/ Lightly spray twelve 6 cm (2½ in) diameter, 2.5 cm (1 in) deep tartlet tins with oil spray. Roll out the pastry on a lightly floured work surface until 2–3 mm (⅛ in) thick. Using an 8 cm (3¼ in) round pastry cutter, cut out twelve discs from the pastry. Line the tins with the pastry, gently pressing it into the sides to fit. Refrigerate for 20 minutes.

4/ Preheat the oven to 165°C (330°F). Line each pastry case with a piece of aluminium foil, pushing the foil to fit the shape of the tin. Fill with baking beans, ceramic balls or uncooked rice to weight down the foil (use enough to fill up to the top of each tin). Blind bake the pastry for 20 minutes. Remove from the oven and gently remove the foil and weights, then return the tarts to the oven for a further 5 minutes to dry out.

5/ Leave to cool, then remove the tins. Melt the chopped chocolate and brush it over the inside of each tart. Reserve until needed.

Red velvet muffins w̲ white chocolate.

On some mornings I crave something sweet, while on others I'd rather something savoury – it all depends on my mood or how busy my day is. Inspired by the classic red velvet cake, these muffins are perfect for 'on the go' breakfast treats. These are definitely for the sweet days.

Chef's tip
Make the batter the night before and pipe it into the muffin holes, cover with plastic wrap and refrigerate overnight. In the morning, simply take the tin out of the fridge, leave at room temperature for 15 minutes while you preheat the oven, and then bake.

Makes
12

Prep time
15 minutes

Cook time
18 minutes

250 g (9 oz/1⅔ cups) plain (all-purpose) flour
30 g (1 oz/¼ cup) Dutch (unsweetened) cocoa powder
2 teaspoons baking powder
170 g (6 oz) caster (superfine) sugar
1 teaspoon salt
2 eggs
185 ml (6 fl oz/¾ cup) full-cream (whole) milk
125 g (4½ oz) unsalted butter, melted and cooled
2 teaspoons red food colouring, or as needed
65 g (2¼ oz) white chocolate chips
Cream cheese frosting (page 11)

1/ Preheat the oven to 170°C (340°F). Grease a 12-hole standard muffin tin.

2/ Sieve the flour, cocoa powder and baking powder into the bowl of a freestanding electric mixer. Stir in the sugar and salt, then attach the paddle.

3/ Lightly beat the eggs in a bowl and stir in the milk. Turn the machine onto low speed and slowly trickle the milk mixture into the bowl, beating until combined well. Add the melted butter followed by the red food colouring, adding enough to reach the desired colour. Continue to beat, then add the chocolate chips and briefly mix until evenly distributed.

4/ Transfer the batter into a piping (icing) bag fitted with a plain nozzle and pipe it into the muffin holes. Bake for 16–18 minutes, or until a skewer inserted into the centre comes out clean. Cool in the tin for 10 minutes before transferring to a wire rack. Leave to cool completely before icing.

5/ Transfer the cream cheese frosting into a piping bag fitted with a plain nozzle. Pipe some frosting on top of each muffin.

Breakfast playlist.

Mornings are all about cranking up the music and getting happy in the kitchen. If you're at home and need some tunes to get your day and breakfast off to the right start, then follow me on Spotify and get my 'Chefs Eat Breakfast Too' playlist pumping through the speakers.

No matter whether you're having a Sunday lie-in with breakfast in bed or in the kitchen flipping pancakes, these are my top ten songs to start the day:

WAKE ME UP BEFORE YOU GO-GO
Wham!

CAN'T GET OUT OF BED
The Charlatans

CORNFLAKE GIRL
Tori Amos

GREY DAY
Madness

I'M GOOD
Wafia

IN THE MORNING
The Coral

BREAKFAST IN BED
UB40 with Chrissie Hynde

IN MY BED
Amy Winehouse

WAKE UP THE NATION
Paul Weller

HERE COMES THE SUN
The Beatles

Finding things.

Thank you.

Early morning thanks to everyone who helped make every day better and brighter, and without whom this book would not have happened.

#teamCEBT

We are on a roll, guys!

Jane Willson

Marg Bowman

Ari Hatzis

Caroline Velik

Vaughan Mossop

Kim Rowney

Elisa Watson

#teamDarrenPurchese

Joe and Samar Chahin and family

Dempsey Smythe – BR Wellington

Roberta Barichello – Printcess

Alexandra Stevens – Burch & Purchese Sweet Studio

Blaze Yiap – Burch & Purchese Sweet Studio

Dewi Utomo – Burch & Purchese Sweet Studio

Kyle Feneley – Burch & Purchese Sweet Studio

Carla Di Felice – Burch & Purchese Sweet Studio

Nichole Horvath – Burch & Purchese Sweet Studio

David Van Rooy – Vanrooy Machinery

Duncan Black – Vanrooy Machinery

James Stone – Vanrooy Machinery

'Scuba' Steve Vaughan

Gary McBean and family – Gary's Quality Meats, Prahran Market

Poh Ling Yeow – Jamface

Mum and Dad

Emma, Ben, Ava, Quin, Harper & Hannah

The awesome crew at LaManna & Sons at South Yarra for supplying all of the amazing produce for this book.

Special thanks to Fifi Box for her awesomely generous foreword. Thanks Fifi. x

Extra special thanks to Christean Ng for all of your support and all the amazing work you do for us. I could not have done this book without you, little almond meal. x

Who's Darren?

Darren Purchese is a sweet man with a savoury side. His Sweet Studio in Melbourne, Australia, is a mecca for dessert lovers and he is known for his devilishly hard dessert challenges on TV's global smash *Masterchef Australia*. What you might not know is that Darren started out as a savoury chef and he especially loves cooking breakfast! Being a pastry chef, he's used to early mornings and this gives him time to indulge in one of his favourite meals of the day, brekkie. Darren shows us perfect eggs, amazing combinations, the ultimate breakfasts from around the world and, of course, some sweet starts to the day with his Bressert section. There is absolutely no truth to any of the rumours that he has stolen all of his wife's, respected chef Cath Claringbold, recipes. They just happen to be similar.

Chefs Eat Breakfast Too is the third book in Darren's *Chefs...Too* series of cookbooks. Stay updated by following us on the social channels below:

Instagram: @ChefsEat

Twitter: @ChefsEatBooks

Facebook: @ChefsEatBooks

Use the #ChefsEatBreakfast hashtag when posting pics of your creations using the recipes from this book, and we will share and repost them.

Published in 2019 by Hardie Grant Books,
an imprint of Hardie Grant Publishing

Hardie Grant Books (Melbourne)
Building 1, 658 Church Street
Richmond, Victoria 3121

Hardie Grant Books (London)
5th & 6th Floors
52–54 Southwark Street
London SE1 1UN

hardiegrantbooks.com

NATIONAL
LIBRARY
OF AUSTRALIA

A catalogue record for this
book is available from the
National Library of Australia

Chefs Eat Breakfast Too
ISBN 978 1 74379 485 2

Publishing Director: Jane Willson
Managing Editor: Marg Bowman
Editor: Kim Rowney
Designer: Vaughan Mossop @ NBHD Creative
Photographers: Ari Hatzis and Elisa Watson
Stylist: Caroline Velik
Proofreader: Charlotte Orr
Indexer: Neil Daly
Design Manager: Jessica Lowe
Production Manager: Todd Rechner

Colour reproduction by Splitting Image Colour Studio
Printed in China by Leo Paper Product. LTD

3 1327 00669 5647